Claire Preston

REAKTION BOOKS

For the Melissae
Elizabeth Flowerday, Laura Gilbert, Sarah Strader, Susan Bridgen,
Lucinda Rumsey, Michelle Shepherd-Barron
and the Bees of England

Published by Reaktion Books Ltd
Unit 32, Waterside
44–48 Wharf Road
London N1 7UX, UK
www.reaktionbooks.co.uk

First published 2006, reprinted 2015
This edition first published 2019
Copyright © Claire Preston 2006, 2019

The publishers and author gratefully acknowledge support
for the publication of this book by the AHRC

Arts & Humanities
Research Council

All rights reserved

No part of this publication may be reproduced, stored in a retrieval system or
transmitted, in any form or by any means, electronic, mechanical, photocopying,
recording or otherwise, without the prior permission of the publishers

Printed and bound in Great Britain by Bell & Bain, Glasgow

A catalogue record for this book is available from the British Library

ISBN 978 1 78914 048 4

Contents

one

The Reasons for Bees

The only reason for being a bee that I know of is making honey
... and the only reason for making honey is so I can eat it.
A. A. Milne, *Winnie-the-Pooh* (1926)[1]

The proverb goes *una apis, nulla apis* – one bee is no bee – and so this book is misnamed. The evolutionary miracle of so-called 'political' insects, with their extraordinary social and biological organization, and remarkable, unique manufacturing and engineering abilities, is the miracle of *bees* together, tens of thousands of bees. The social sentience of all these bees seemed to the ancient world, and until quite recently, a moral sentience. And the moral life, as Thomas Hobbes wrote, is the life *inter omnes*; it is the life of bees.

Our planet teems with bees, about 20,000 apian species in all, most of them indispensable to plant ecology. But the cultural history of bees overwhelmingly features just one of these – *Apis mellifera*, or the western honeybee. The honeybee, alone among animals, *makes* something by a kind of craft out of elements external to itself. Compare the bee to the silkworm and the cow: the latter naturally produce substances from their bodies which, harvested by man, are used or converted for use into fabric and food. The meat and skins of the animals we hunt and rear for food are constituent and integral to them: they cannot live without their fur or their muscles, nor can they make anything from them. But the bee's main product, honey, is its own finished and complete manufacture, which it fabricates from gathered raw materials. Unlike silk and milk, honey is a behavioural artefact of the artisanal civilization of bees. In some ways honey has more in common with the serviceable talents of horses and dogs in performing tasks than it has with cheese and sausages and cloth from the bodies of cows and silkworms. The ant and the termite, the two other families of social insect, display the same high organization and specialization, but only the honeybee's exemplary behaviour also generates to mankind products of great use and value. The bee was technically among the first domestic animals, but, as if to retain mastery of its products, it has never been, strictly speaking, domesticated. For all their social graces, bees are essentially wild.

Bees and men have been acquainted with each other during the whole of human history. The bee, a far older species than the bee-keeper, was operating in its astonishing patterns of civil behaviour before mankind had evolved anything resembling social organiza-tion. When eventually he turned into a social animal, he learned to rob wild bees, then to kill hived ones and, at last, to pilfer politely from them, almost as if the purpose of bees on earth were to teach man the ways of enlightened self-interest and how to behave fairly and reasonably.

Because of its immensely long history in association with man, the bee has been more carefully observed, more celebrated, more storied and mythologized, and latterly more feared than most other animals. Some of the first pictographic human records include business with bees, as do the earliest written ones. From the first Greek poetry to the latest Hollywood horror film, the bee stands as an emblem of man's relation to nature and to himself. The mystery and the wonder of the bee prompted the

One of the earliest anatomical studies of the bee using a microscope, from Francesco Stelluti, *Persio tradotto* (1630).

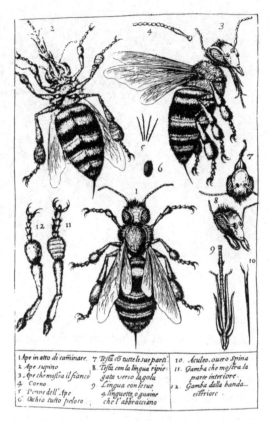

1 Ape in atto di caminare.	7 Testa cō tutte le sue parti.	10. Aculeo, ouero Spina
2 Ape supino	8. Testa con la lingua ripie-	11. Gamba che mostra la
3 Ape che mostra il fianco	gata verso lagola	parte interiore.
4 Corno	9 Lingua con le sue	12 Gamba dalla banda
5 Penne dell'Ape	4.linguette, o guaine	esteriore.
6 Occhio tutto peloso	che l'abbracciano	

seventeenth-century scientists who used the earliest, primitive microscopes to describe and draw the bee before all other creatures.

Bees are everywhere. But despite their huge geographical range, their cultural territory is relatively limited. Most of the extensive mythology and symbolism of bees arose and ramified in the Judaeo-Graeco-Christian West for the simple reason that the European honeybee in its various subspecies is both the most prolific producer of honey and temperamentally the most adaptable to domestic cultivation. In those non-western parts of the world – southern Africa and the Indian sub-continent – where an old apian cultural

Eckfeldapis electrapoides, a fossilized ancestor of the modern bee, from Germany, *c.* 50 million years old.

tradition exists, it is one of bee-hunting rather than of domestication, and consequently yields less elaborate visions of apian society and behaviour than those regions where hived bees were readily and consistently observed.

Apis mellifera originated in southern Asia (probably in and around Afghanistan), but there are surprisingly few Far Eastern bee traditions to examine, possibly because the phenomenon of the sweet tooth appears to be a western and northern one, and in many Asian cultures there was relatively little demand for honey. Although the western honeybees were imported to South America in the 1530s, the Maya of Meso-America had long since domesticated the stingless bee (of the subfamily *Apidae Meliponinae*) and incorporated it into their myths and records; and there are no native North American legends concerning honeybees, which were only imported in 1621 to Virginia (by the Dutch) and known to the native Americans as 'the Englishman's fly'. Thus, lest it appear otherwise, this book does not wilfully or carelessly exclude non-western traditions in favour of a Mediterranean, European focus. It is the bees themselves who have flourished there.

In the bee's rich history some interesting paradoxes emerge. The perception of one apian quality – selflessness – informed much ancient and early-modern bee-mythology: as the quintessence of civility, the bee works always for the common good, and can no more be bribed or corrupted than a flower. The bee is Nature's workaholic. In the post-industrial era, however, that same selflessness in the form of mass behaviour has yielded the horror of the mindless, monstrously violent, Bacchic swarm which irrationally and unpredictably attacks the defenceless individual. Bees themselves are of course in thrall to a natural imperative which is no more generous or public-spiritedly selfless than the survival instinct of any other animal; but this has been interpreted as mechanical subjection to inscrutable higher powers. For this reason the bee has been a favourite of social satirists and political polemicists. Indeed, the ideologues of power think of bee-keeping as the appropriation of the labour of oppressed worker bees, and of bee-keeping as a form of enslavement.[2] This book will follow those contradictory ideas in history, where fear of the masses competes

Mayan bee icons.

with virtuous group undertakings, where individuality and self-determination seem threatened by the collective will.

A related contradiction is the conception of the bee as, on the one hand, publicly oriented, part of a complex, highly evolved hierarchical commonwealth, and on the other, private, modest, secret, retiring, unindividuated, seeking no more than to be an anonymous and identical cog in a wonderful natural machine. Thus the bee is associated with both public *and* private virtues: the bee stands both for the outer-directed life of social benefit as well as the ancient and attractive convention of retirement from public life. Hobbes's dictum that 'the Common good differeth not from the Private',[3] that the retired individual has a civil role within the communal life of the nation, is central to the myth of the bee. That myth also promoted a slightly different form of retirement among its admirers. When Sherlock Holmes gave up detection, he went to the country, there to produce at leisure a *magnum opus* entitled *Practical Handbook of Bee Culture, with some Observations upon the Segregation of the Queen*.[4] George MacKenzie, praising contemplative solitude in England during the Restoration years after 1660, cited the solitary Phyliscus, 'a great Philosopher, that for fifty years . . . employed himself in the observation of Bees', that most social of animals.[5] Those country persons learned in bee-lore around Concord, Massachusetts, seemed to Henry Thoreau to have garnered a kind of natural wisdom: 'I love best the unscientific man's knowledge; there is so much humanity in it.'[6] James Fenimore Cooper's lonely American frontiersman and honey-hunter finds pleasing civic morals in the life of bees, and remarks: 'I often think of these things, out here in the wilderness, when I'm alone, and my thoughts are actyve [*sic*].'[7] For each, public virtues and public behaviour are best considered in retirement, in the company of bees.

The honeybee as artisan, and the virtues of honey itself, have a folkloric and theological tradition. In discussing certain symbolic features of the natural world, Claude Lévi-Strauss places bees and honey transitionally between nature and culture: as 'wild' bees are nonetheless markedly civilized, so raw food – the natural, the primitive, and the untamed – is artificially converted by cooking into the edible, the domesticated. In this analogy, bees are cooks, foraging for unadulterated nectar and converting it by chemical and thermal processes into honey. Even if it is unclear whether the South American tribal understanding with which Lévi-Strauss was concerned was sufficiently advanced to analyse the honey-making process and to make such an analogy (for some South American tribes, honey was a vegetable because it was found in trees),[8] it is interesting that bees feature in fundamental Warao, Parana Guarani and Tupi creation myths in which bees feed infant gods, just as they do in the Greek tradition, and that bees are associated with the godhead (wasps issuing from the deceiver-figure), as in Christian fable, and other origin myths from around the world feature bees. Indeed, the very first adventure of that brainless bear Pooh – an origin myth in its own right for the '100 Aker Wood' – was a famously bear-brained attempt to steal honey from some bees by means of a dodgy blue balloon. Needless to say, the bees – cleverer than any bear – were not fooled.

In the western tradition, honey stands for eloquence, immortality and sheer pleasure: the infant Plato, left by his parents on the slopes of Mount Hymettus near Athens, was fed by bees who put honey into his mouth so that his utterances were ever afterward like honey dropping from his lips. The poet Pindar was likewise said to have had honey fed to him by bees as he slept,[9] and the same tale is told of Sophocles, Xenophon, Virgil, Lucan and St Basil.[10] St Ambrose of Milan (340–397) and St Bernard of Clairvaux

St Ambrose as
a wicker-woven skep.

St Ambrose, styled
'doctor mellifluus',
was a patron saint of
beekeepers.

(1090–1153) were styled doctor mellifluus ('honey-flowing doctor')
on account of their sweet rhetoric. Ambrose is often depicted with
a beehive, Bernard with a swarm of bees; both saints are patrons
of beekeepers, bees, candlemakers and wax-melters and refiners,
and St Valentine and St Modomnock of Ireland (a beekeeper) are
also sometimes associated with beekeepers. Democritus asked to
be buried in honey at his death, probably because as the first
practical anatomist he knew that it is an excellent preservative for
organic specimens (he would not, of course, have known why:
honey's high osmolarity – its ability to draw off moisture – and its
antibacterial enzymes prevent decay and infection). Herman
Melville paid honey the whaleman's highest compliment: other
than to be 'coffined, hearsed, and tombed' in fragrant, delightful
spermaceti,

only one sweeter end can readily be recalled – the delicious death of an Ohio honey-hunter, who seeking honey in the crotch of a hollow tree, found such exceeding store of it, that leaning too far over, it sucked him in, so that he died embalmed. How many, think ye, have likewise fallen into Plato's honey head, and sweetly perished there?[11]

This seventeenth-century epigram, entitled 'Plato', connects the mellifluous and the preservative: 'Those bees, which chose thy sweet mouth for their hive, to gather honey from thy works, survive.'[12]

The health of ecosystems can be judged partly by the health of bees, an intimation surely accounting for the great stores of honey in heaven and the promised lands of most eschatologies. The Qu'ran promises rivers of it in paradise;[13] the heavenly Jerusalem of the Jewish tradition is environed with fountains of it; the Puritan settlers in Massachusetts Colony revived the biblical promise of milk and honey for their people in the New World even before there were bees there to provide any.

But these vignettes of eloquence, retirement, philosophy, delightful death, and salvation associated with the bee are far from the creature itself. Unless there is pleasure in dying of overwork, bees are anything but distractible by pleasure: as a character in a recent novel remarks, 'You could not stop a bee from working if you tried.'[14] They are neither sentimental nor romantic; nor are they philosophical, although they inspire philosophers; nor do they retire into contemplative solitude. One bee is no bee, so almost none of the standard western ideas of individuality and autonomy of self have any purchase in the study of bees. One bee, indeed, is no bee at all, 'but a multitude of Bees uniting their forces together, is very profitable, very comfortable, very terrible – profitable to their owners, comfortable to themselves, terrible to their enemies.'[15] *Bees* are always communal, plural, public, unindividuated, corporate, *en masse*. 'Fame's a motive which they never feel; Their ruling passion is the public weal,' wrote a late-eighteenth-century admirer.[16] Their entire organism – mechanical, endocrinal, behavioural – is evolved solely to function as an interchangeable part in the natural, efficient factory known as the beehive. Maurice Maeterlinck tells us that 'the bee is above all . . . a creature of the crowd . . . isolate her, and however abundant the food or favourable the temperature, she will expire in a few days not of hunger or cold, but of loneliness.'[17]

What we admire and fear in the bee is that anonymity: the equally powerful impulses in western psychological organization – individuality and social belonging – are essentially at odds and the bee offers an apparently reassuring example of complete social integration. To *observe* the bee, however, offers us the occasion of solitude, individuality and retirement. Anyone who has ever watched bees going purposefully about their tasks will have admired the severe beauty of their single-mindedness and will immediately guess why they have so deeply moved philosophers, writers and artists. The valiant undertakings of these tiny creatures, who seem to house large hearts in little bodies, are in aid of apparently wholly beneficial ends – the bee carries her own weight in nectar and pollen, and literally works herself to death; her ragged wings, after only a few weeks of life carrying out perhaps 1,000 flower-missions a day, show her age and imminent end. Coupled with the extreme vulnerability of her delicate ecostructure to environmental conditions, the bee's labour is marvellous and beautiful. And yet anyone who has ever been the victim of an apparently unprovoked bee-sting will ruefully dismiss the age-old folly of anthropomorphizing bees, who so easily and falsely seem to conform to human ideas of behaviour and intention.

Osip Mandelstam's vision of bees unites some of these oppositions:

Take from my palms, for your delight and joy,
A little honey and a little sun,
As Persephoné's bees commanded.
The punt unmoored cannot be untied,
The furry shadows cannot be discerned,
Nor life's incessant terror surmounted.

What's left to us, is only a kiss –
The kisses bristly like the little bees
That die the moment they desert the hive.

They rustle in night's transparent jungles,
Living on time, meadowsweet and mint –
The children of the forest of Taigetos.

Take for your joy my present, simple and wild –
Uncomely, shrivelled necklace
Of bees that die transforming honey into sun.[18]

In speaking of his poetry, Mandelstam invokes the almost magical process by which bees convert sunlight into honey and honey into candlelight, a process tinged by the melancholy selflessness of the spent bee whose dead, used-up body reminds us of the cruelly mortal miracle whose evidence is honey. Mandelstam's bees (which appear frequently in his work) retain some of their ancient symbolic heft: they are wise as they were in Greek legend, and linked with various earth-deities, notably Demeter and Persephone. The sacramental quality of their conversion of one substance into another (ineffable sunlight into sticky sweetness, and honey back again into sunlight) recollects the holy medieval connexion of bees with Christ; and the final resurrectionary line suggests the old belief in the bee as the embodiment of the soul returning to heaven. The poem – on the nature of poetic creation itself, an art of converting the ineffable (thought and experience) into words – buzzes and hums, as many of Mandelstam's poems do, with the mental ambience of inspiration which the poet sacramentally converts into language: 'Everything chirps and rocks,' he says elsewhere. 'The air quivers with comparisons.'[19]

These indefatigable insects, who build their combs and collect their nectar just about anywhere, have colonized our cultural landscape just as thoroughly as they have done our physical world. Our history of thinking about ourselves quivers with bees. The comparisons we have made depend on our understanding – inventive if often misguided – of the natural history of the creature itself.

two

Biological Bee

The bee was intended to live in the midst of an indifferent
and unconscious nature.

Maurice Maeterlinck, *The Life of the Bee* (1924)[1]

Nothing in the astonishing mythology of the bee – the
tales of its amazing social design, its piety or valour
or wisdom – is as miraculous as its biology. A member
of the order Hymenoptera, Section Aculeata (those insects whose
females have stings), a bee belongs to one of approximately 20,000
species within this group which form the superfamily Apoidea
(the other superfamilies of Aculeata include those of the wasp
and the ant). Apoidea includes all the 'social' or 'political' insects
except the termites[2] – that is, it includes almost all those insects
whose colonies contain workers and other individuals with
specialized abilities which, in combination, allow the colony to
reproduce, gather and/or manufacture food and extend its range
successfully. The colonial behaviour of some bee-species – the feature which has allowed them to become in a sense 'domesticated'
– is among the most complex of any animal.

Contrary to ancient folklore, however, most species of bee are
not social; those few that are – members of the subfamilies Apinae
and Meliponinae – are also the ones which produce large quantities
of honey, and have thus been most interesting to mankind. Within
the subfamily Apinae, and the genus Apis, the species *Apis mellifera*

('honey-bearing bee' – a misnomer) is the scientific label of the common western honeybee, which occurs indigenously or by human introduction all over the world. But this name, given by Linnaeus in 1758, is misleading: bees do not carry honey from flowers at all, but partially produce it within their honey-sacs and store it in the hive. Linnaeus recognized the error and tried to re-christen the species *Apis mellifica* ('honey-making bee'), but the rules of taxonomy have since determined that the first given name takes precedence, so it is the older name that is still used.[3] *Apis mellifera* includes the subspecies of the western and the African honeybee, with the darker brown Caucasians and the Carniolans, and the lighter yellow Italians (said to be the most desirable to bee-keepers for their easy temperament and rigorous work habits) as 'races' of the western honeybee. Although native to Eurasia, the honeybee has flourished throughout the world's temperate zones, and especially in the New World and Oceania where no native honeybees exist. Other indigenous honeybees include African races of *Apis mellifera* and the Asian species Apis cerana and the giant honeybee, *Apis dorsata*. These last three groups are, either because of their lower productivity or their unmanageability, less well adapted to temperate zone apiculture, the source of nearly all thinking about bees. This is another reason why much of this book is decidedly Eurocentric.

The bee has, in common with all insects, a membrane-jointed, six-legged exoskeleton; but unlike most other insects in Apoidea, which have shiny, smooth chitinous carapaces, bees are fuzzy with hairs that catch pollen. The worker bees and the queen have stingers that pump venom into the victim; the stinger of the honeybee is serrated and cannot easily be withdrawn from flesh, so that the bee disembowels itself in order to fly away, and dies shortly afterward. A honeybee can, however, sting the fleshless

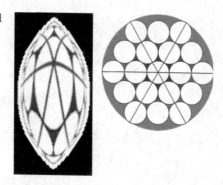

The diamond-shaped image represents the distortion made by the bee's compound eye.

exoskeleton of another bee and survive. Some other species of bee can sting repeatedly.

The bee has an unusually large brain (1 mg) for its size, in comparison with most other insects; in addition to its brain it possesses ventral ganglia which control much of its motor activity, so that a decapitated honeybee can fly, walk and sting, although it cannot perform any of the social tasks governed by the brain. Its compound eyes vary in size and function according to the caste of bee: the biggest eyes belong to the male drones, who must locate the queen on the wing during her nuptial flight; the smallest are the queen's, who will probably spend her whole life in the comb laying eggs.

Bees make various sounds – for example, the piping of virgin queens as they prepare to emerge from their cells, the warbling of the nurse-bees when they are producing more 'bee-milk' than can be consumed by the larval bees, and the hissing of the workers when the wall of the hive is knocked – and these are all produced by the exhalation of air from the spiracles (or ling valves) on the thorax. The wing-beat frequency of the hive, if detectable, is an excellent warning system indicating the imminence of a swarm, and Edward Farrington Woods MBE, a war-time English beekeeper, invented an electronic 'apidictor' to alert beekeepers of what was

Tanging the bees by beating on metal implements, from Virgil's *Georgics*, illustrated by Wenceslaus Hollar (1691).

about to happen, although the patented device was not a commercial success.[4] But bees have no known auditory equipment beyond the ability to sense surface motion and the oscillation of air-borne particles, and the purpose of these utterances is so far unknown. Thus, various extremely ancient and persistent superstitions about 'tanging' the bees (calling them by beating on metal implements) are almost certainly meaningless. Even if the bee cannot hear, its two antennae contain powerful sense-organs for touch and smell. It discriminates among the surface structures of flower-petals, and can detect fragrance. Recent research suggests that it possesses a plastic sense of smell – that is, that for the bee shapes have fragrance. Its sensitivity to electrical fields accounts for its agitation before storms. Like many other animals, bees can sense the earth's magnetic field, which they use in navigation and perhaps in comb-building. Gravity, however, is not apparently very significant in these activities: tests on bees by NASA aboard a shuttle mission showed that their ability to reproduce and to construct combs was unimpaired by weightlessness.

A variety of striped yellow, brown and black members of the wasp family, such as hornets and yellowjackets, are often mistaken for bees. Wasps, however, are carnivorous and eat not only other insects (including bees), but also rotting meat and fish. Like bees, they gather nectar and are attracted to sweet substances like fruit, but they do not make honey. The wasp's nest, which, like the bee-hive is composed of cells for rearing larvae, is a fragile, papery construction rather like a Chinese lantern made of wood pulp and saliva. It is abandoned each autumn because virtually all the wasps other than a few overwintering queens die off. Wasps can both bite and sting, and can do so repeatedly.

Unlike the carnivorous wasps, adult bees are nourished entirely on honey made from nectar, pollen and water. In order to gather these substances, the worker bee's proboscis has become specialized and longer than those of the drones or the queen. As a bee gathers nectar from flowers through its proboscis, it sends it either to the alimentary canal or to the honey-sac, which share a valve. But gathered nectar is rarely eaten directly by the foraging bee, who feeds instead on honey already manufactured in the hive. The process of converting nectar into honey begins, however, in each bee's honey-sac, where it is mixed with an enzyme, invertase, which starts to transform the raw nectar's sucrose into dextrose (glucose) and levulose (fructose), a process which continues in the comb.

Pollen, highly proteinaceous, is eaten by young bees and is essential for the development of the larvae. The honeybee's fur collects pollen inadvertently as it enters the flower blossom, but some bumble-bee species, which have a proboscis too short for certain blossoms (such as those of the tomato and other vegetables and fruit), have extended the possibilities of pollen collection by evolving as 'buzz pollinators'. At middle C, according to investigators, their vibration shakes the pollen down onto their fur, to be carried to the hive. Bees internally manufacture other enzymatic foods – royal jelly and bee milk – to feed to larval bees.

Its highly social organization has evolved to allow the honeybee to carry out the large-scale manufacture of honey to support a reduced colony over the winter; a colony which, come spring, will re-start the work of the hive. Large amounts of honey require storage and defence systems, and the many tasks involved in

The queen's retinue, from William Cotton, *A Short and Simple Letter to Cottagers from a Conservative Bee-Keeper* (1838).

The queen's retinue, from Wilhelm Busch's *Buzz a Buzz, or The Bees* (1872).

making, storing and protecting honey have promoted exceptional specialization in bee labour. The hive is divided between a single adult queen and the tens of thousands of morphologically distinct female 'worker' bees who are her offspring. The queen is constantly attended by a retinue of worker bees who feed, clean, cool and warm her so that she can efficiently carry out her sole function in the hive, the laying of eggs. The female workers do all the remaining work of the colony.

The far less numerous drone bees ('Unprofitable and harmfull Hangbyes'[5]) are the only males in the colony; they too are the queen's offspring, but their single function is to mate with her, and once this has occurred (or, as in most years in a successful colony, if their services are not required at all), they are driven out of the hive by the worker bees to die of starvation. This exclusion of some hundreds of drones each autumn is one of the most remarkable sights in the animal kingdom. The workers are pitiless: drones do no work in the maintenance of the colony and cannot even feed themselves, so they cannot be allowed to overwinter and consume precious resources.

The most talented specialists are the workers. They are the builders, brood-nurses, honey-makers, pollen-stampers, guards, porters and foragers, and these tasks are related to their developmental age. All worker bees, in other words, take up these functions in succession as they mature, with the newest workers undertaking nursing, cleaning, building and repair in the nest, somewhat older workers making honey and standing guard, and the oldest bees foraging for pollen and nectar. Although the queen can live for up to four or five years, the worker bees normally live four or five weeks in the summer, or as much as a few months if born late in the season and destined to overwinter. Although a recent neurological study by Professor Rudolf Menzel seems to suggest that bees are a good deal lazier than we have been led to believe, that they rest themselves when they could be working harder, this supposition is based on the unreasonable expectation that they ought to work at night instead of sleeping. In truth, the bee is visibly worn out by her work after only a few weeks, and the writer Paul Theroux, himself a serious beekeeper, defends the creature: 'I've seen them dancing, I've seen them faffing about in the honey, and I've seen them grooming the queen, but I've never seen them bunking off.'[6]

These three castes of bee are co-dependent: the queen and the larval bees cannot survive without the workers to support them; the queen cannot produce workers without a drone; the drones cannot support themselves; the workers cannot reproduce, except when no queen exists, and then the offspring of laying workers are drones (a situation catastrophic for the colony). Other bee species, such as bumblebees, are less symbiotically organized: the bumblebee queen is morphologically similar to her workers and begins the life of the colony as a solitary worker performing all the functions of the hive until she can produce workers to assist her and a division of labour can be established. Unlike honeybee colonies, which produce and store excess honey to support a diminished but still quite large population over the winter, all bumblebees, except for a few virgin queens, die off each autumn, and their colonies must be established *ex nihilo* each spring. Still other kinds of bee are merely communal, with two or more queens sharing a nest; and there are further 'quasisocial', 'parasocial' and truly solitary bee species.

A typical, successful artificial honeybee hive will have anything from 40,000 to 100,000 bees in it, all of whom are the offspring of the queen. Wild colonies are likely to be smaller. The queen honeybee in a natural or wild state has a single 'nuptial' flight early in her life (commercially produced queens, however, are artificially inseminated and are never allowed to make this flight). In the nuptial flight, a newly hatched queen replacing a dead or swarmed predecessor takes to the air trailing sex pheromones, an event which summons all the drones from her own and from neighbouring hives. Each drone who catches her will mate with her on the wing, a union which will disembowel him. She receives during this flight a lifetime's complement of sperm which she stores in her spermatheca and which she will use during the whole of her reproductive life. Thus all the bees in the hive at any given moment are either half or full siblings, with various father-drones represented in the queen's spermatheca. Returned to her nest, she lays about a thousand internally fertilized eggs a day for the rest of her life directly into wax cells produced by the workers within the hive, and about the same number of adult bees hatch every day. These fertilized eggs will almost all develop as infertile female worker bees. A few of the worker larvae will be reared as queens in case the old queen becomes infertile, dies, or leads a swarm out of the hive. The very few unfertilized eggs will become fertile male drones. All of these hatch as larvae which are subsequently fed on the glandular

The nurse bees, from Busch's *Buzz a Buzz, or The Bees*.

secretion of young nurse bees called 'bee milk'. The worker bee larvae which are to be turned into potential queens by the nurse-bees are specially reared in larger cells and are fed on another of the worker's glandular secretions, royal jelly. All the larvae, of whatever type, grow enormously quickly and are sealed into their cells after several days, where they spin their cocoons and begin to pupate. When fully formed as adult bees (after two or three weeks, depending on the caste of bee) they break free of their pupal skin and gnaw their way out of their cells.

A great many of the tasks of the workers are governed by the secretion of different enzymes. The youngest bees secrete bee-milk from the hypopharyngeal gland, and royal jelly. This enzymatic secretion ceases after about ten days, and the nurse-bees move on to other tasks. Slightly older bees secrete scales of wax from between their abdominal plates (a single bee is capable of producing half her own weight in wax during this stage of development) to build and repair the comb. The oldest bees leave the nest to forage (up to two or three miles away), and they can produce the invertase that begins the conversion of nectar and other sweet substances they collect into honey. All workers, as well as the queen, produce venom from the moment of hatching, although baby bees are too

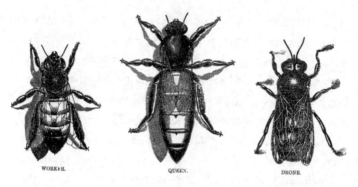

WORKER.   QUEEN.   DRONE.

The three castes of bee: worker, queen and drone; from A. I. Root's *The ABC and XYZ of Bee Culture* (1908).

soft for some days after birth to be able to use their stingers. The highly specialized nature of these various functions very strongly marks the organization of labour within the colony, and, though chemically driven, such a variety and variability of labour would seem at times to require some form of communication between individuals. Pheromones allow bees to identify fellow workers, to mate with the queen, to call foraging bees back to the hive, to attack intruders, to swarm, and to encourage retinue behaviour. But the ability of bees to decide, for example, to build extra honey-storage cells in the hive as needed in years of abundant honey-flow may be only partly based in the production of pheromones, and it is as yet unexplained. It is, however, well established that bees have a language of dance by which they share precise information about the location of pollen and nectar. These dances, which have been minutely studied, appear to convey ideas of distance and direction of food sources.[7] Swarming bees (those looking for a new nest site with their queen) are also guided by such dancing by scout bees who locate and report on the new site.

Bee habitats cover nearly the whole planet, with the exception of Antarctica and the northern ice cap. Bees live below sea-level, even underground in the case of some bumblebees, and are found as high as 3,500 m in the Himalayas. The different European races of honeybee have marked behavioural differences, tending to become less gentle and more ready to sting the farther south they live, Mediterranean and north African subspecies being somewhat more aggressive than northern and western European ones, and the sub-Saharan races more so than any other. All honeybees will defend their nests by stinging; but the aggression of the African varieties is a hive-defence mechanism which has evolved into en masse attacks against predators, which include not only humans but ants, wasps, moths, mice, bears, monkeys, birds and honey-badgers. These African subspecies of *Apis mellifera* have some racial variations among them, but they are not so pronounced as those of the European races, owing to the lesser isolation and disruption of bee migration in the tropical zone during the last ice age.

three

Kept Bee

Bees are creatures full of wonders, being not altogether tame,
nor absolutely wild, but between both, yet indocible,
for most they do is by instinct.
Moses Rusden, *A Further Discovery of Bees* (1679)[1]

T hat the words for honey and for mead, the drink made
from it, share a single root (*medhu-*) across the range of
Indo-European languages and beyond indicates the
early and primary importance of honey in the human diet. It is no
accident, then, that these languages coincide, broadly speaking,
with the temperate areas of the Old World where the western
honeybee and its near relations evolved and proliferated. 'Mead'
is *mede, medd, med, medu, mjod, met, mjöd, miodh, madh, mádhu*
and *methu* in Dutch, Welsh, Czech, Anglo-Saxon, Russian,
German, one of the Scandinavian languages, Irish, Hindi, Sanskrit
and Greek. The related root for 'honey' (or nectar) has an even
broader linguistic range: *milit, mez, mesi, mit, mitsu, mi, mil, miele*
and *mel* in Hittite, Hungarian, Finnish, Tocharian (Scythian),
Japanese, Chinese, Sino-Korean, Italian and Latin. The word for
bee is more varied – the Aryan and Germanic roots bai and beo
have no connection with the Greek *api* – possibly because ancient
peoples were robbers and not keepers of bees, and had more sense
of honey than of the creature itself beyond its sting. Mesolithic
rock-paintings in caves at Bicorp and Barranc Fondo, near Valencia,

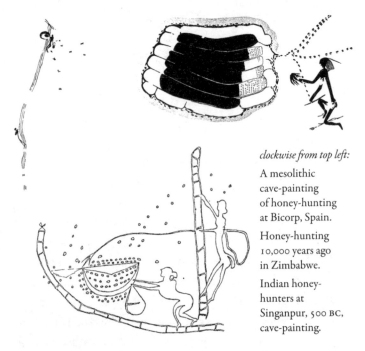

clockwise from top left:
A mesolithic cave-painting of honey-hunting at Bicorp, Spain.
Honey-hunting 10,000 years ago in Zimbabwe.
Indian honey-hunters at Singanpur, 500 BC, cave-painting.

show honey-hunters at work 6,000 years ago, and in many regions of the world honey-hunting, rather than cultivation, remained the primary means of obtaining it until relatively recent times. Mead (or metheglin) – made from fermented honey – is the oldest alcoholic drink known, and it is likely that the promise of alcohol and sweets prompted man to begin keeping bees in artificial hives more than 4,500 years ago.

Apiculture originated in the Mediterranean near-east. The Egyptians, cultivating the North African subspecies *Apis mellifera. lamarckii*, were practising sophisticated apiculture by 2500 BC, and left pictorial records of their craft, which included, by the third century BC, the transporting of hives to different regions for pollination according to annual flooding patterns. The pharaoh Rameses III (1198–1167 BC) gave immense offerings of honey to the god of the Nile; and the hieroglyph of the bee was the symbol of the land and of the ruler of Lower Egypt. The Egyptians used honey as food, as medicine, for embalming and for tribute; beeswax, too, was used as medicine, in storage and preservation, as well as in magic rites.

The practices of beekeeping spread throughout the Near East. It was the Hittites who left the earliest written records of beekeeping (*c.* 1300 BC) which include severe legal punishments for honey thieves.[2] In the Homeric era (*c.* 800 BC), Greek honey was wild honey. By *c.* 750 BC, however, the *Theogony* of Hesiod refers to artificial hives in some detail, and his *Works and Days* alludes to the indolence of the drone. Legal records of the seventh and sixth centuries BC contain laws relating to beekeepers, and Aristophanes (fifth century BC) has characters who are honey-merchants. Bees

The bee symbol of Lower Egypt, from a bas-relief at Karnak.

Hindu bee symbols: Vishnu on a lotus-flower and Siva.

were closely observed by Aristotle (fourth century BC), who believed that honey fell from heaven; and discussed by Pliny (first century AD), who said it was the saliva of the stars or else some kind of juice in the air.[3] Even if the Greeks did not correctly understand what bees do, they eventually became sophisticated beekeepers, using knowledge imported from their eastern neighbours. Several reported works on bees and beekeeping by Theophrastus (fourth century BC) and Nicander (second century BC) are now lost, but the tradition was extended by the Roman writers Varro, Virgil and Columella, of whom more will be said later.

The most ancient Indian sacred work, the *Rig Veda* (a text based on oral tradition originating in the period 3000–2000 BC), refers often to bees and to honey and honey-hunting. There is, however, no record of developed beekeeping in India in this period. Honey-taking from wild bees was an important religious practice associated with the Hindu cults of Vishnu, Indra and Krishna, gods born from nectar and sometimes symbolized by the bee. Similarly, in the ancient records of China there is little about apiculture; as late as AD 983, Li Fang described systematic honey-hunting but not beekeeping.[4] The seventeenth-century writer Samuel Purchas could report, however, that the Chinese of his own era 'wonderfully delight in keeping of Bees there, there is also very much wax, you may lade ships, nay Fleets therewith'.[5] Sophisticated techniques in apiculture no doubt spread across western and northern Europe with the expansion of the Roman empire, but honey-hunting and beekeeping were already well established in the provinces long before that. Understanding of bees, which was connected with the large-scale brewing of mead, became inflected by the Roman tradition, and that hybrid set of ideas survived until the Enlightenment.

They have been likened to grazing animals by recent commentators, to 'lilliputian livestock – fuzzy herbivores with wings'.[6] Bees graze, rather like cattle; they accept some human intervention but do not depend upon it; in winter the surviving bees of the colony crowd together in a dense ball within the hive to generate heat, and each bee in turn works its way slowly toward the centre and back again to the periphery like herd animals in a snowstorm. But if bees have some of the instincts of the herd, they are nevertheless not precisely *domestic* animals. Fortunately, they consent to inhabit artificial hives which have been devised for them, and their relationship to man is better understood as symbiotic, with each species benefiting from certain behaviours and capabilities of the other. What beekeepers do is less like farming and more like ranching – perhaps like lobstering in New England – where conditions are made attractive to an essentially wild species which is consequently induced to behave efficiently for the keeper. The object of beekeeping is to encourage the bees to produce and store surplus honey for the winter which can be taken without compromising the viability of the colony. Thus, the proper housing of bees, the promotion of good honey-making conditions, and the convenient harvesting of their honey are the main concerns of all beekeepers.

All the western bee races are characterized by their habit of making elaborate nests in which they raise workers and store honey against the winter months. A colony of bees will make as much honey as it possibly can. When storage room runs out (either because of overall constraints of space or because the bees are not building new comb fast enough), or the number of bees becomes too large for the site, a 'primary' swarm consisting of a very great proportion of the existing bees will issue from the nest with the queen to establish another colony and start the process again. The much diminished population that remains will throw more of its energies into hatching a new queen and rearing a brood to replace the departed swarm rather than into the collection of nectar and the production of honey. It is only when the population is again robust that the bees return to making surplus honey. Swarming is thus not in the interests of the beekeeper, and even less so if the departed swarm cannot be trapped and housed in another hive. In the wild, moreover, nests proliferate inconveniently and unpredictably from the point of view of the honey-gatherer, who has to locate them and go to considerable trouble to liberate the honey, and at the cost of destroying a good set of combs. It is in the bees' interest to have their honey taken in a non-destructive manner (although they do not recognize that they are cooperating with the beekeeper in this sense). It is the keeper's aim to keep the honey in one place by encouraging the bees to remain in or near the original nest. This is done by providing them with more room to breed and store (which is done by extending the space of the

A horizontal hive from a medieval *exultet* roll.

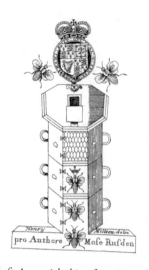

Left: An upright hive, from Moses Rusden, *A Further Discovery of Bees* (1679).
Right: A woven skep.

hive as needed) so that excess honey can be removed in the late summer or early autumn, leaving the bees with enough to survive the coming winter months. If a colony should swarm, a beekeeper will try to provide the travelling bees with a new hive nearby which can also be controlled, and a stray swarm which has landed on a branch with its queen can usually be captured by an experienced keeper, who will be glad to acquire a new colony and offer it a home in an empty hive.

Until the modern era, in the arid regions of the Middle East, North Africa and southern Europe hives were constructed of baked mud, pottery, bricks, dung, cork, logs, wicker, mica and horn, which were usually horizontal, with the combs hanging vertically along the length of the hive. In the northern forested areas of Europe, where wild bees settled in hollow trees, beekeeping originated in artificial cavities made in trees, and from this vertical axis developed the upright hives of the modern era in transalpine regions. The hive in these areas – constructed of logs or of wicker or other woven materials and known as 'skeps' – assumed the classic beehive shape of the inverted goblet. The keeper had only to lift the skep and cut the comb out.

Until about 1500 the process necessitated the killing of the bees by smoke; but the unanswerable economics of preserving rather than destroying successful colonies soon produced the escape hatch, so that in the more technically sophisticated hives the bees were only temporarily evacuated. In general, however, the practice of killing bees persisted until well into the nineteenth century, and beekeeping manuals of the Renaissance and later periods are much concerned with the issue of killing bees. The technique of smoking the hives non-lethally, however, brilliantly capitalizes on the natural behaviour of bees. Although it is often assumed that the keeper's smoke makes the bees drowsy or chases them away, and a nineteenth-century writer advocated the use of pulverized puffball fungus which did actually stun the bees without harming them,[7] the truth is that it makes them respond as if their hive were on fire: they quickly prepare themselves to flee by gorging themselves with honey (their travelling provisions); when their honey-sacs are full they cannot manipulate their stingers effectively and are temporarily harmless. Modern keepers use this opportunity to add medicine to the smoke which combats mites and other parasites.

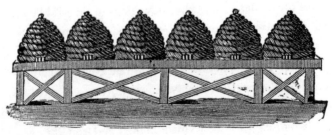

Woven skeps, from William Cotton, *My Bee Book* (1842).

Above and above right:
Victorian multiple
hives, from Edmund
Evans, *Bee-Keeping*
(1864).

Right: The Greek
top-bar hive, from
George Wheler,
*A Journey into
Greece* (1682).

The Greek Beehive

The bee's own highly structured behaviour and social organization makes very slight interventions and adjustments by humans inordinately effective: from earliest times we have found ways of encouraging bees to do better what they already do quite naturally. So, although a few very useful technical improvements have been made to the efficiency of honey production and harvesting – mainly in the architecture of the skep – the essential methods of beekeeping have changed little over the millennia. The seventeenth-century invention in England of the tiered-frame beehive (which allowed the keeper to add 'supers' or extra storeys for the building of honeycomb) improved the quantities of honey that could be harvested. The discovery of a Greek style of primitive movable-frame hive was an even more important innovation: because bees must naturally attach their combs to some solid structure, the keeper was obliged to cut the combs away from the inside surface of the

The Langstroth Hive.

hive in order to collect the honey. This destroyed the comb for future use. The Greek hive's movable hanging combs (attached to horizontal bars) allowed the combs to be removed without cutting, and prompted the bees to create a larger series of combs within one skep. The Greek model was used by English beekeepers to improve the standard vertical northern European hive by adjusting the size of the artificial tiers to suit the size of specific bee-species. Nevertheless, bees also tend to caulk their hives with wax and propolis (a very sticky, hard-drying plant-resin which they collect from flowers), and even with the Greek hives beekeepers struggled with the age-long difficulty of wresting the comb away from the hive walls with as little damage as possible.

The year 1851 was the *annus mirabilis* of beekeeping. In that year, the Revd Lorenzo L. Langstroth of Philadelphia, with the simplicity of real genius, devised a new hive which created a 'bee-space' (about 35 mm) between the hive wall and the frame edge, a space he determined by years of observation, which the bees respected and did not attempt to bridge with a wax or propolis joint. Thus was born the modern beehive, whose hanging frames of honey-filled combs rest in slots and can be readily removed

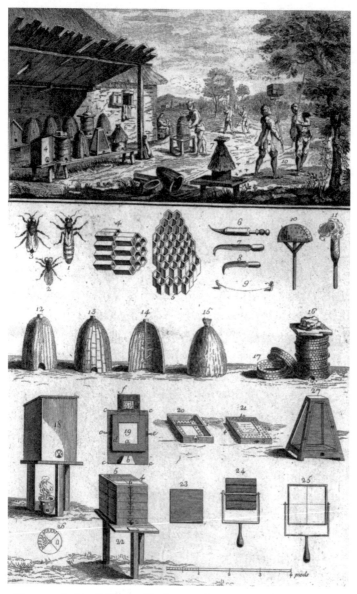

The art and science of bees and beekeeping, from Denis Diderot, 'Economie Rustique' in his and Jean d'Alembert's *Encyclopédie* (1751–72).

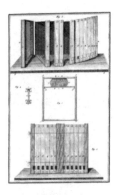

Left: A leaf-hive, from François Huber, *Nouvelles observations sur les abeilles* (1792).

Right: 'Work That Educates': a 1914 photo from the US National Child Labor Administration showing John Spargo, a Vermont beekeeper, and his 12-year-old son.

almost like hanging files from a filing cabinet as they are completed by the bees, to be emptied by the keeper and replaced in the hive. The double-sided combs become more or less permanent, once constructed. All modern hives descend, so to speak, from the Langstroth innovation. A slightly later invention – hexagonally embossed wax 'foundation' onto which the bees can attach the double-sided cell-structure – saves them even more energy. The modern beekeeper, unless particularly wishing to make beeswax products, can uncap the sealed honey cells (by gently scraping off the tops) without wholly destroying the comb or cutting it away from the frame. After centrifuging the combs and extracting the honey, the movable frame with its intact, emptied comb can be left outdoors, where the bees will find it and thoroughly clean it by salvaging any remaining honey. When it is replaced in the hive, the bees have merely to repair it rather than build it again from scratch. This allows them to spend more time making honey and making fresh comb for it, and not a drop of honey is lost to keeper or bee.

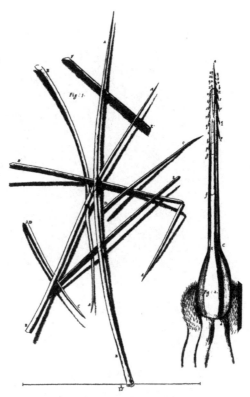

The stinger of a bee magnified in Robert Hooke's *Micrographia* (1675).

These and subsequent developments in beekeeping have promoted the health of bee populations (their most serious modern enemies are the varroa mite and the tracheal mite), and better extraction systems for collecting honey from the wax combs have enhanced the beekeeper's ability to prosper and extend really efficient and high-producing colonies.

When the Italian prince Federico Cesi and his colleague Francesco Stelluti, members of the Accademia Lincei in Rome, first studied and drew the bee under a microscope in 1625, what they saw astounded them. The invention of high-resolution magnifying lenses in the late-sixteenth century allowed observers to see, for

TAB. XX

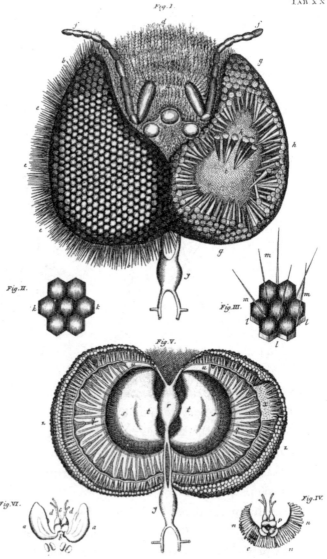

The bee's compound eye magnified, from Jan Swammerdam,
Biblia Naturae (1737–8).

the first time, the anatomy of an animal supposedly familiar to mankind from earliest times. 'Hee that would behold the shoppe [chops] of a bees mouth,' Thomas Browne wrote in the 1650s, 'may behold one of the rarest artifices in nature.'[8] The findings of Malpighi, Cesi, Stelluti, Hooke, Swammerdam and Leeuwenhoek eventually confirmed, in spite of two millennia of error, that the queen bee is female and lays all the eggs, that the workers are female, that the drones are male, that the workers produce wax. Even so, an intensely practical seventeenth-century apiarist could publish an authoritative book on the subject which insisted that the drones are not male and have nothing to do with the conception of new bees, that the head-bee is not female, and that bees breed without copulation, but instead, as Aristotle believed, that they gather 'animable matter' (e.g. pollen) and mix it with the sperm of the king bee in various ways to produce the different castes of bee.[9] And until about 1800, the true origin of all the substances associated with honey-making – bee-brood, beeswax, nectar, honeydew, pollen and propolis – was not entirely understood. The belief that bees feed on dew, or that they gather honey from plants, that they produce honeydew, or that they are born from honey generated a rich body of folklore and pharmacopoeia. It was only the eighteenth-century investigators who were finally able to show that nectar and propolis are plant- not bee-products, and that honeydew is produced by aphids.

'A Bee is an exquisite Chymist', said Charles II's Royal Bee-Keeper.[10] Apian chemistry is indeed remarkable. The worker bees forage among flowering plants for nectar, pollen and propolis. The nectar is converted into honey, first by the addition of enzymes during the digestive process within the bee's honey-sac, and then by evaporative desiccation in the hive, which radically reduces the regurgitated nectar's naturally high moisture content and makes it into a supersaturated sugar solution. The bees fan their wings to produce body heat, which gives the hive an ambient temperature of about 95°F/35°C. This is also the warmth needed to hatch the larval bees. The adult bees maintain this temperature in different weather conditions by fanning or water-cooling. And their stored-up treasure is precious: a pound of finished honey (0.45 kg) requires 55,000 miles of bee travel to produce it, but a high-producing hive can produce as much as two pounds of honey every day in an abundant year. Even though a single bee can gather up to a teaspoon of nectar every day in the course of a thousand flower-visits, her life's work amounts to just a quarter of a teaspoon of finished honey.

Most foraging bees gather nectar or other sweet liquids, but some specialize in gathering pollen, which all bees gather willy-nilly on their furry coats as they rummage for nectar inside flowers. They comb the pollen from their fur during flight using the brush-like comb joints on their hind legs; they then form it into tiny balls using a little nectar, to be stored in the so-called 'pollen-baskets', or depressions in the bee's hind legs, and delivered to the hive. A fully pollen-loaded bee seems to be wearing enormous yellow or orange plus-fours or saddle-bags, and can easily be spotted at the entrance of the hive. Honey and pollen are unloaded from the forager by house bees and stored in the combs as food for the working colony and for larval and newly hatched bees. Bees also prize honey-dew (a nectar-like secretion of aphids and plant-eating scale insects, the original manna of the Israelites), which they also gather and make into honey, but they will collect almost any sweet liquid if given opportunity; this is why, like wasps, they often hover around ice-lollies, sweet drinks and fruit, and assiduously attend, though uninvited, the garden parties and playgrounds where these are on offer. Other than these gathered substances, they produce wax, extruded from glands in the young bee's abdomen and used to construct combs, and the queen produces bee-brood (larval bees), an excellent source of protein for nest-robbing animal predators and considered a delicacy in a number of Asian cuisines. The other substance processed by bees is propolis, a resinous plant substance, which is gathered from vegetation and used as an adhesive for nest repair.

Scientific work on bees did not much influence practical beekeeping until the mid-nineteenth century. Although occasional intersections occurred between disinterested and pragmatic work with bees – such as Dr Wilkins's glass beehives in the gardens of Wadham College, Oxford, in the mid-seventeenth century – the practices of beekeeping remained more or less unchanged, despite economic incentives to increase and improve production. Wilkins's glass 'observation' hives were clearly a great wonder – even the

John Evelyn's sketch of his glass observation hive obtained from Wadham College, Oxford.

King visited them – and John Evelyn, the diarist and practical innovator, was shown them in 1654, but his delight in them was as much aesthetic as pragmatic: '[Wilkins] shew'd me the transparent apiaries, which he had built like castles and palaces and so order'd them one upon another as to take the honey without destroying the bees.'[11] The hives had dials, weathervanes, and decorative statuary, like elaborate garden ornaments (which they were). Wilkins gave Evelyn an empty hive, which he took back to his own garden at Sayes Court, Deptford, on the eastern edge of London. Samuel Pepys came and looked with interest and approval at Evelyn's prized possession: 'you may see the bees making their honey and combs mighty pleasantly', he noted.[12] Being able to see his bees at work may have formed Evelyn's views on beekeeping in *Kalendarium Hortense* (1669): help your bees kill their drones in July, he advised; put honey beer in front of the hive to distract marauding wasps.[13] As tiered wooden hives were introduced and replaced the traditional woven skep, Robert Plot, the Oxford naturalist, remarked in his survey of such improvements, 'Of Arts relating to Brutes, I have met with none extraordinary concerning the winged Kingdom, but the new sort of boxes, or Colony hives for Bees.'[14]

Sugar had been steadily supplanting honey in European cookery since the early-sixteenth century, and it was this expensive reliance on imported cane sugar from the West Indies, Brazil and India, rather than on cheaper native honey as a sugar source, that interested seventeenth-century social visionaries like Samuel Hartlib, who advocated developments in efficient northern apiculture for honey and wax, as well as improved orchard keeping to benefit bees and fruit and the making of cider (conceived as the national drink). Bees and cider were to promote trade, prosperity, health and national virtue. Even elite writers like Sir Kenelm Digby and John Evelyn produced recipes for mead and other

Observation hives, from Antoine Réaumur, *Mémoires pour
servir a l'histoire des insectes: les abeilles* (1740).

honey-based drinks as part of their programme for national and
individual self-sufficiency.

Today the average British consumption of honey per capita is
0.66 lbs (0.3 kg), in America it is 1.1 lbs (0.5 kg), in Germany an
extraordinary 9.5 lbs (4.3 kg).[15] Compared with refined sugar intake
(currently 30–40 kg per capita in the industrialized west), modern
beekeepers are not producing an essential commodity, cheap cane-
and beet-sugar supplying most of the world. No longer the primary source of sweetener, honey in the western world has instead
become an alternative sugar-source with some well-established
health benefits, and a luxury food with various flavours, organic
guarantees and hand-made attributes contributing to its gourmet
glamour. Because it takes on flavours from the plants of which it
is made, regional and 'varietal' honeys are marketed like wine,
with descriptions of flavour, viscosity and colour, and by appeal
to styles, as well as to the sense of locale, exclusivity, natural whole-
someness and craftsmanship. Because of this, a quasi-technical and
official palette of honey colours based on the Pfund Scale (a colour-
measurement system devised originally by the glass industry)
ranges from 'water white', 'extra white' and 'white' through 'extra

light amber', 'light amber', 'amber' and 'dark amber'. Commercial American honey varietals are rated by the US Department of Agricultural Statistics Service, which has adapted these colour-terms for its annual honey report:

borage (a dark honey)
tulip poplar (dark red amber, distinctive yet mild)
alfalfa (white or very light amber)
buckwheat (dark and pungent, tasting of molasses and malt)
pima cotton (very light)
fireweed (clear with a delicate tea-like flavour)
manzanita or bearberry (white to light amber, tangy and
    berry-flavoured, popular with chefs)
snowberry (water clear or white; granulates slowly, so it
    stores well)
pumpkin (strong flavour, amber)
sage (rich light, clovery and floral)
tupelo (complex, floral, herby)

Such variety has spawned a profitable market in 'premium' and 'super-premium' honeys, and the positively poetic advertisements for them give a good impression of the way in which bees and their product have been used to promote a nebulous enthusiasm for the handmade, the 'natural' and the rare:

Gourmet is proud to exclusively offer the super premium honeys from Il Forteto, whose bees collect pollen from the idyllic fields around Mugello in Northern Italy. This area is rich in tradition and has always been the foremost game pre-serve in the Italian countryside.

Acacia honey . . . is great drizzled lightly over a bit of pecorino or gorgonzola . . .

Pure rosemary-dominant flora honey originates from the Alentejo region of Portugal. This is a rural and sparsely populated region where nature, man, and culture live in symbiosis in an ecologically preserved environment.

But 'the pedigree of Honey does not concern the Bee', as Emily Dickinson curtly remarked.[16] Like much advertising, the one thing 'designer' honey ads lack is anything factually relevant to the making of honey by bees. They don't make honey from pollen in Mugello (or anywhere), nor are they swayed by the 'rich traditions' or the 'idyll' of the area or the density of its population. Bees work happily in the largest cities and in construction sites. But snobbery and meaningless appeals to fuzzy notions of cultural and natural symbiosis and 'ecological preservation' are standard elements in the branding of honey, which is designed to be aspirational by invoking attractive notions of artisanal 'authenticity', the glamour of foreign locales, and the sophistication of larders with 'bits' of gorgonzola loitering in them as a matter of course. 'Gourmet' [sic] honeys are also sold with additions not known to bees – white truffles, hazelnuts, and other expensive items. American honeys also cash in on the appeal to exclusivity. Tupelo honey, unusually high in fructose, is made from the flowers of the tupelo tree and widely valued as one of the world's best honeys. Like a fine wine with its own distinctive terroir, it is produced commercially only on the banks of the Ochlockonee River near Savannah, Georgia.

In America, where arable acreage is usually extensive, continuous and monocultural, large commercial beekeeping operations are likelier to derive their main income not from honey but from

The Co-operative Society's beehive emblem, set into one of their buildings.

the pollination services of the bees themselves. Substantial colonies of honeybees and other species, depending on the crop, are transported, usually in special stackable palettes loaded on trucks or trains, to regions where large-scale efficient pollination is required. The almond growers of California require the seasonal services of imported bees, as do the blueberry farmers of Maine, and certain bee races are naturally adapted as the best pollinators of certain types of flowers. In Europe, where acreage is more condensed and broken up, large pollination operations are less common. European bees often work under glass or plastic (for example, on strawberries), and on apricots and other fruit trees in open ground in places like Provence. They are sometimes assisted by special pollen inserts, devices placed at the hive entrances to dust the emerging bees, who then deliver the pollen in the field. European growers have been especially active in specializing bees for particular crops. For example, bumblebees are very effective buzz-pollinators of tomatoes, aubergines, potatoes, peppers, blueberries, watermelon and cranberries; and they work better than honeybees in greenhouses and plastic tunnels, because unlike honeybees they do not become disoriented and lose their way home (most bumble-bees are troglodytes, or underground-dwelling, which may account for their talent indoors). But bumblebee colonies consist of far fewer individuals than honeybee colonies, and their numbers decline rapidly in the course of a pollination season, making them in this respect harder to manage as pollinators.

Honeybees pollinate a very large range of agricultural crops (as many as 95 in the United States), but other bees are valuable agricultural workers: the leafcutter bee pollinates alfalfa; bumblebees work in commercial greenhouses growing cucumbers and tomatoes; the orchard mason bee works in fruit trees. Nevertheless, the handmade aura which surrounds honey and makes it so attractive to organic farmers and to the faddists of the 'all-natural' has been cleverly co-opted by the pollinating concerns: one successful Maine-based company, Bee Here Now, combines the funky counter-culture allure of its name with a thriving commercial pollination service which extends as far south as Georgia. There are an estimated 2.59 million artificial bee colonies in the United States, with an average yield per colony of 69.9 lbs (31.7 kg), and many of these are commercial. Beekeeping, however, also survives with vigour as a hobby and as the produce of small-holdings by keepers with under ten colonies.

We no longer require the essential benefits of honey and wax on which earlier societies depended, and so bees no longer generate quite the same ideas of efficiency and order they once did, in the time before the secrets of plant reproduction, pollination and interspecific symbiosis were discovered. But those old ideas are latent in our modern sense of the bee, and for modern beekeepers, commercial and private, who daily witness the sturdy economy of their hives, the ancient political meaning of bees is not quite lost.

four
Political Bee

For where's the State beneath the Firmament
That doth excell the Bees for Government?
Guillaume de Salluste Du Bartas,
La Semaine; ou, Creation du Monde (1578)[1]

An ancient and vibrant set of apian political and moral emblems produced assumptions about the sex of various categories of bee and about their social organization, some of which survive in the present. A well-known Renaissance emblem (employed for personal use by Sir Philip Sidney, among others) shows a swarm of bees with the motto *Non nobis* ('not for ourselves', adapted from *sic vos non vobis mellificatis apes*, 'so do you, bees, make honey, but not for yourselves'). The unstated corollary of this expression of apian altruism, 'not for ourselves', is 'instead, for others'. The bee nation was perceived to cooperate as a group of comrade-members, a communist commonwealth in which the individual subsumes herself in the collective enterprise and good of the colony, and each bee acts for the general benefit of all the other bees. In the civil nation of bees,

By hoarded wealth no individual tries
Above the modest citizen to rise;
No sordid av'rice taints the gen'rous mind;

Non nobis.
An emblem from
George Wither,
*A Collection of
Emblemes* (1634–5).

Their stock in common lies to all resigned;
And when in civil compact they unite,
No state is so observant of the right.[2]

Their household virtues were held to include parsimony,
cleanliness, unaffected taste, tameness and tractability, nobility, gen-
erosity, modesty, industry and valour,[3] and they were praised for
their united sensibility ('when one is sicke, they all mourne').[4] This
charming view of the apian character and polity originates with the
Greek poet Hesiod, who uses bees as examples of diligent agricultural activity, and condemns both women and sluggards by analogy
with drones.[5] Bees 'detest the lazy', says Varro, and so annually kill
the drones, who do no work and only eat up the precious supplies
of honey.[6] 'Tis industry our state maintains,' says an angry, virtuous
bee to a luxurious, corrupt one in John Gay's *Fables*.[7] 'Such enemies
are they to idleness' that elderly bees unable to work were said to
refuse food.[8] In discussions of suicide, the bee was cited as an example
of 'deserting oneself Lawfully': 'by the Law of Nature it self, things
may, yea must, neglect themselves for others, of which the Pelican
is an Instance. Another Instance [is] Bees ...'[9] The Hispano-Latin
agricultural writer Columella devotes an extensive chapter of *De
Rustica* (a guide for husbandmen) to the care of bees, with the clear
implication that a well-ordered apiary full of virtuous bees is the

Virgil's osier bridge for bees, from the *Georgics*, illustrated by Wenceslaus Hollar.

sure sign of a frugal and attentive farmer. Columella deems 'perfect honesty' necessary in beekeeping because bees 'revolt . . . against fraudulent management.' The idea has persisted, even in modern culture, that an orderly and successful hive reflects the virtue of the keeper, and only the virtuous can keep bees.

The great *locus classicus* for the moral bee, and the source of *non nobis*, is Virgil's *Georgics*, poems about the farming and agricultural practices of the imperial Romans. The fourth section of *Georgics* is a delightful mixture of practical beekeeping tips (make little bridges of osiers across brooks, he instructs, so that bees can drink

'A Vision of Virgil', from Wilhelm Busch, *Buzz a Buzz, or The Bees*.

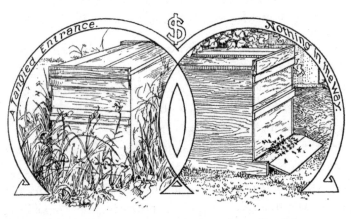

'Profit in bees', from A. I. Root, *The ABC and XYZ of Bee Culture*.

The Bee Hive department store in Patchogue, New York, 1958.

easily), and descriptions of their social and political life. Virgil's bees are surprisingly democratic, having developed a disinterested political system and legal code designed to provision the populace and secure the future of the state rather than to promote the interests of particular individuals. 'All's the state's; the state provides for all', says Virgil.[10] Although his bees have a (male) leader, his is an elected office, and he can be removed if proved unsatisfactory. Virgilian bees have a highly evolved society in which the young and lusty male bees are the soldiers and the workers, the female bees raise the infant bees and keep the nest clean, and the oldsters stay at home to teach young bees their lessons. Most interesting of all Virgil's conceits is that of bees as commercial creatures, their hive the 'busy shop' and the bees themselves 'trading citizens'.[11] This commercial bee lived a long cultural life and could still be invoked in 1832 by Frances Trollope, who informed her readers that Cincinnati, Ohio, was a town where 'every bee in the hive is actively employed in search of that honey of Hybla, vulgarly called money'.[12] The commercial bee of Virgil is imagined by Henry David Thoreau as a prosperous and hardworking Yankee burgher with negotiable business interests:

> The rambler in the most remote woods and pastures little
> thinks that the bees which are humming so industriously on

the rare wild flowers he is plucking for his herbarium, in some out-of-the-way nook, are, like himself, ramblers from the village, perhaps from his own yard, come to get their honey for his hives . . . I feel the richer for this experience. It taught me that even the insects in my path are not loafers, but have their special errands. Not merely and vaguely in this world, but in this hour, each about its business. If, then, there are any sweet flowers still lingering on the hillside, it is known to the bees both of the forest and the village. The botanist should make interest with the bees if he would know when the flowers open and when they close.[13]

The Virgilian bee-fantasy was constantly retold or adapted for the next millennium and a half. The Emperor Trajan, wrote Plutarch, studied Virgil's account 'that he might borrow a civil life

'The Discovery of the Business End of the Bees' on a poster for Charles Yale and Sidney Ellis's play *The Evil Eye*, produced at the St John (New Brunswick) Opera House in 1899.

Andreas Alciati, 'Ex bello pax', *Emblematum Liber* (1531).

from Bees'.[14] Seneca, the mentor of Nero, likened the apian polity (perhaps ironically) to a benign monarchy, and instructed his young protegé Lucilius to copy the behaviour of bees.[15] Anxiety in the early-modern period about political and social disorder made the bee a constant example of efficiency and careful government, and so writers of the English Renaissance admired bees especially for their strictness in enforcing labour and their practical good government: 'how just they are,' wrote Godfrey Goodman, 'in putting those statutes in execution, concerning idle persons and vagabonds, and likewise the employment of the day-labourers.'[16] A well-known Renaissance emblem shows bees nesting in a knight's helmet, with the motto *ex bello pax* ('out of war comes peace').

'Divers beasts', William Allen wrote in the late-sixteenth century, do reach unto [government], in their congregations and common wealthes, as is to be seene among emetts [ants] and bees ... that by instinct of nature are sociable, and do live in company and consequently also do maynteyne so much order and pollicy in that common wealth, as is needful for that preservation and continuance.'[17] Shakespeare resorts to the Virgilian tradition near the beginning of *Henry V*, when he illustrates with apian 'order and pollicy' the new king's development not only of a belligerent and glorious adventure against the French but also the establishment of the tenor of his reign, which is to be quite distinct from the chaotic regime of his father:

> For so work the honey-bees,
> Creatures that by a rule in nature teach
> The act of order to a peopled kingdom.
> They have a king, and officers of sorts,
> Where some like magistrates correct at home;
> Others like merchants venture trade abroad;
> Others like soldiers, armed in their stings
> Make boot upon the summer's velvet buds,
> Which pillage they with merry march bring home
> To the tent royal of their emperor,
> Who busied in his majesty surveys
> The singing masons building roofs of gold,
> The civil citizens lading up the honey,
> The poor mechanic porters crowding in
> Their heavy burdens at his narrow gate,
> The sad-eyed justice with his surly hum
> Delivering o'er to executors pale
> The lazy yawning drone.[18]

The bee represents order, evidence of 'rule in nature', a systematic framework of obedience that promotes peace. But was the bee colony a monarchy or a republic? Was it a matriarchy or a patriarchy? What were its laws, procedures and punishments? Could bees offer political solutions to troubled human government? The elaborate social development of bees produced some fantastic

The crowned king bee, from Richard Daye, *The Parliament of Bees* (1641).

THe Parliament is held, Bils and Complaints
Heard and reform'd, with feverall reftraints
Of ufurpt freedome ; inftituted Law
To keepe the Common- Wealth of Bees in awe.

notions of their intellectual and ethical powers. Thomas Moffett, an important sixteenth-century naturalist, was persuaded of the extensive civilization among bees described by Virgil, whose fable he improved in describing their conduct of wars and of councils, the passing of laws and the carrying out of civic punishments. Apian duties, according to Moffett, included regimental guard-duty, physick, burial and trumpeting.[19] His bees are certainly monarchists who mourn the loss of their king with 'tragicall lamentation', even though, because 'they are swayed by sovereignty, not tyranny', they will not scruple to execute a king bee who 'make[s] his lust the rule of his Government'; and if he is a merely negligent king they will crop his wings until 'he amend his manners'.[20] The exclusion and death of the drones had long been observed by naturalists, a phenomenon which Moffett interprets as the strategic weeding out of competing noble factions. Like others, he found his bees modest,

The king bee dominates in this monument to Grand-Duke Ferdinando I of Florence, 1608, Piazza della S. Annunziata, Florence.

especially in copulation (certainly because their true reproductive behaviour – the laying of already-fertilized eggs by the queen – was not recognized), fond of 'simple and unaffected' music, and full of household virtues. Thomas Browne noted their construction of sepulchres for their dead and their elaborate exequies.

The etymology of the word 'bee', it was claimed, conveniently derived from a Dutch word for 'ruler' or 'king'.[21] The 'king' bee was said to be twice the size of other bees, 'his thighs straight and strong, his gait loftier, his aspect more stately and majestical, and on his forehead a white spot like a shining Diadem or Crown'.[22] English Royalist writers of the sixteenth and seventeenth centuries co-opted these highly attractive and orderly ethic, economic and political virtues into their own propaganda promoting obedience to a divinely established ruler. There was much debate as to the sex of the head bee: by 1586 it was recognized that she is female, but it was Charles Butler who first published this news in England in 1609. The hive, he said, was 'an *Amazonian* or *feminine king-dome*' where 'the males ... beare no sway at al';[23] and in retrospect, this fact was offered as a powerful natural precedent for Elizabeth I's reign. But these writers were often interested less by the bee's natural altruism than by its obedience. Moses Rusden, as might be expected of a Royal Beekeeper, claimed bees were proof that 'Monarchy is founded in Nature', since 'such ingenious, laborious and profitable Creatures do voluntarily and constantly betake themselves to that Government'.[24] The annual exclusion and death of the drones and the killing off of spare queens, moreover, dem-onstrated that bees 'abhorre as well polyarchie, as anarchie, God having shewed in them unto men an expresse patterne of a perfect monarchie, the most natural & absolute forme of government'.[25]

More severely Protestant writers than Rusden, as well as the theorists of the Cromwellian Commonwealth, with their own sects and parties structured around a presbytery or an appointed leader, found in the bee more of the old Virgilian merits of coop-eration, equal standing and mutual benefit, and established the head bee through natural sovereignty ('goodliness, goodness, mildness, majesty') rather than by lots or heredity.[26] The courtesy writers, too, advocated the civility of bees as a model for human comportment; and the scientists of the seventeenth century were

The golden bees found in the tomb of the 5th-century AD Merovingian monarch Childeric I.

particularly attracted to this model, with their large Baconian enterprises requiring concerted efforts from many individuals. Even so, the Virgilian model of the civil bee was subject to revision and extension. So distinguished a naturalist as Robert Hooke could speculate that the bee's sting, which he studied through a microscope, was proof that 'Nature did realy intend revenge.'[27] As political animals, bees also bore the weight of satire. John Levett warns in his beekeeping manual of the danger of drones, who are 'necessary and helpfull to the Bees, so long as they exceed not a due proportion (much like to our Lawyers), but let their number grow to[o] great (as it often doth) and they will indeed devoure the substance of the Bees (as the Lawyers of the Commonwealth) and bring it to destruction'.[28] In Levett's apian universe, the Master Bee has regal authority, 'correcting the lazie, sloathfull, and disobedient, and giving honour and incouragement to those which are painfull, laborious, and diligent'.[29]

The bee as political example was extended by leaders who adopted it as an armorial sign. The French Republic already being symbolized by the beehive, and wishing to establish himself with an emblem more venerable and possibly less autocratic than the royal *fleur de lys* of the Bourbon kings he had displaced, Napoleon chose bees to recognize the tiny golden ones discovered in the tomb of

The Napoleonic bee in an imperial escutcheon on a tapestry.

the Frankish king Childeric I (*d.* 481) when it was opened in the mid-sixteenth century. The bee might also have proposed itself in subtly alluding to, but not replicating, the shape of the *fleur de lys*. Some old French families already featured the bee in their armorial bearings to represent their civic duty to king and people, and Joan

The Barberini trigon in Francesco Stelluti's 1625 engraving for *Melissographia*.

of Arc was represented with a beehive to signal a female leader defending her kingdom: her banner was said to carry the motto *Virgo regnum mucrone tuetur* ('A virgin defends the kingdom at the point of her sword').[30] The Barberini family which dominated Rome and the Vatican in the seventeenth century chose a trigon of bees as their heraldic emblem, and the accession of a Barberini to the Papal throne in 1623 prompted the experimental philosophers of the Accademia Lincei to celebrate with three scientific treatises on bees, *Melissographia*, *Apes Dianiae* and *Apiarium* (1625). *Melissographia* was published with an engraved title-page showing anatomically exact bees in the form of the Barberini trigon.

In our own era, Les Murray has ironically alluded to the old argument of 'natural' monarchy in his poem about Australian republicanism, 'The Swarm' (1977). The 'English' bees he observes in a settled swarm are 'Poor monarchists, clumped round their queen' with tattered wings, 'clenched loyalists' who mindlessly repeat '*Some eat the royal jelly: / most do not. This is Right. Work and die.* What is, is ...' The beekeeper is figured as a Royalist who soothes the potentially rebellious, escaped swarm with his smoke pot, and captures it for his hives.[31]

A more homely, commonsense bee tradition existed alongside the specifically political ones: Samuel Hartlib, writing in 1655, wistfully notes that 'old and young bees do live quietly in the same Hive, as did the families in the old world', almost as if he were lamenting the troublesomeness of the modern human teenager.[32] These rather puritanical bees are not only sexually modest (and cannot tolerate being handled by a beekeeper who has not abstained from sexual relations for at least the prior 24 hours),[33] but also 'cannot anywise endure' foppery in humans, and are especially annoyed by the wearing of perfume, curled hair and red clothes.[34] Bees are inclined to be friendly to those who are chaste, clean, neat, plainly dressed and not 'sluttish', but are given to stinging those who are sweaty, suffer from halitosis (particularly from pickled fish, onions, or garlic),[35] breathe heavily, or are drunken.[36]

Aesop tells the story of some drones who discovered a hive full of honey and made war on the bees to whom it belonged. The

Lucas Cranach, *Cupid Complaining to Venus* ('The Honey Thief'),
c. 1530s, oil on wood.

Venus comforting Cupid after he is stung by bees (Andreas Alciati, *Emblematum Liber*, 1531).

battle became too heated and a wise wasp was called in to judge the matter of ownership. The wasp declared that each party should produce some new honey, and whichever specimen tasted most like the disputed honey would indicate the rightful owner. The bees readily accepted this proposal, but the drones refused, whereupon the wasp concluded that they were unable to make their own honey and awarded the hive to the bees. The bee and the just man were often compared,[37] but although bees are usually righteous, they can occasionally overdo it: in another fable, Aesop tells the story of the bees and Zeus: the bees, having presented Zeus with a vessel of honey, were offered a wish in return by the pleased god. The bees asked that their stings, when used against hive-robbers, should in perpetuity be mortal. This request displeased Zeus as entirely unreasonable and extreme, so he decreed that any bee who used its sting would itself die.

Bees are highly instructive when they appear in moral tales. Theocritus first told the story of Cupid's encounter with bees. In this satisfying episode of the biter bit (and a regular subject of

Renaissance emblems), Cupid is either trying to steal honey, or just generally trespassing on bee territory, as retold here by Robert Herrick:

Cupid as he lay among
Roses by a bee was stung.
Whereupon in anger flying
To his Mother, said thus crying;
Help! O help! Your Boy's a dying.
And why, my pretty Lad, said she?
Then blubbering replyed he,
A winged Snake has bitten me,
Which Country people call a Bee.
At which she smil'd; then with her hairs
And kisses drying up his tears:
Alas! Said she, my Wag! if this

Albrecht Dürer, *Cupid Complaining to Venus*, 1514,
pen and ink and watercolour on paper.

Filips von Marnix, *De Roomische Byenkorf* ('The Romish Beehive', 1581).

Such a pernicious torment is:
Come, tel me then, how great's the smart
Of those, thou woundest with thy Dart![38]

Moral and political bee lore is, perhaps inevitably, subject to local manipulations. Although the skep-shaped pontifical mitre must have given sixteenth-century Protestant polemicists the hint which converted the orderly Virgilian beehive into the evil nest of 'Pharasaical Frie' which was the Romish church,[39] Dryden, with evident relief, emphasizes in his late-seventeenth-century translation of Virgil's *Georgics* that the common bees can check the whims of their 'high-flying arbitrary kings' by clipping their wings.[40] John Daye in *The Parliament of Bees* (1697) uses apian social organization as it was then understood to devise an anti-Jacobite harrangue: 'whaspish *Bees*' stand for 'murmuring, caballing, & assassinating Regicides', while the right-minded bees elect to choose a king who will govern in the true Protestant religion.[41]

$45 bill with beehives from the 1779 Republican Congress in Philadelphia.

Although Isaac Watts's little busy bee energetically 'improves each shining hour',[42] John Gay's satirical fable 'The Degenerate Bees' tells of an uprising of 'luxurious, negligent' bees who sow corruption in the hive by indulging the selfish instinct for wealth and power. The few honest bees who stand up to them point out 'that in selfish ends pursuing, / You scramble for the public ruin.'[43] The honest bees are dismissed from the hive but predict its return to right governance. Dedicated to Jonathan Swift, the fable is an encomium of honesty, fearless forthrightness and cooperation.

This conventional set of anecdotes about bee society could become all but reflexive and meaningfully exhausted, as in Bernard Mandeville's *The Grumbling Hive* (1705) (later rewritten as *The Fable of the Bees* (1714)), an elaborate satire on early-eighteenth-century English commercial and political developments which only invokes bees as cynical members of an extended social organization, without drawing on specific apian characteristics or behaviours. The place of the bee in the period of the American and French revolutions is, however, distinct and explicit: the American enthusiasm for the austere economic virtue of bees was perpetuated by Emily Dickinson, in a poem laconic even by her own severe standards:

Partake as doth the bee,
Abstemiously;
A rose is an estate
In Sicily.[44]

The civic and political virtues long established in the Virgilian bee tradition put the beehive on the paper money issued by the American Republican Congress in 1779, and probably gave the hint to the French republicans of the next decade. Symbolically significant beehives such as a nineteenth-century Capitol building continue as an American kitsch fashion, and there is a theme park in the form of a twee little Bee City in South Carolina which looks like the MGM backlot of the 1930s; it includes a Town Hall hive, a Hospital Hive and a Barber Shop hive called 'Buzz Cuts' (because 'everyone has the right to be neat and trim'). Beeswax figurines and

The Capitol, Washington, DC, as a beehive (A. I. Root, *The ABC and XYZ of Bee Culture*).

Bees in revolt against an inquisitive child are observed by a young woman wearing the Phrygian cap of the Jacobins in this print from 1850.

Egalité with a Republican skep (Pierre-Paul Prud'hon, *Egalité*).

sculptures marketed on the Bee City website – of the Last Supper and Mother Teresa – continue to connect the virtues of bees with Christian icons of righteousness while celebrating their distinctively economic tendencies. American affection and respect for bees is hardly surprising: the War of Independence, for all its grand rhetoric about the rights of man, began as a dispute about taxes.

French Revolutionary bee propaganda is more clearly Virgilian and political. Among its republican symbols were the skep and

The French Revolutionary beehive.

hexagon, denoting the community of workers and the rough geographical outline of France itself. In the illustration opposite, the tablet engraved 'the Rights of Man' is stationed next to a skep. It may have been this tradition that prompted François Mitterrand

A Revolutionary beehive by Ian Hamilton Finlay.

to call his political memoirs of the late 1970s 'The Bee and the Architect'.[45] Arthur Murphy's *The Bees* (1790), a translation of Vanière, carefully apologizes for offering so uninteresting a subject when the public mind is distracted by 'the wild ambitions of the French anarchists', but goes on to describe the emerging new queen bee as consulting with 'the friends of revolution', and the pillaging wild, woodland bees as radicals who 'raise contributions, new republics plan, / And [call destructive] force "THE RIGHTS OF MAN".' It was published with a tract of the same year called *The Necessity of Destroying the French Republic*.[46] The political French beehive prompted English commentators to take up the apian theme. In 1792 Mary Alcock, in response to the trial of Louis XVI, suggested that 'in these degenerate times / Insects have learn'd from man to ape their crimes.' The bee ceases to be an emblem of social order and good governance and becomes convulsed by revolution. Her fable tells of a hive taken over by rebellious bees who insist 'Let all be equal', and who buzz 'of liberty, no work – the rights of bees'.[47]

The tone of these political bee fables has changed over the past two centuries to meet the ideology of the moment. In *Liberty Lyrics*, published in 1895 by the Anarchist Communists, bees are congratulated for being free of masters, money, the press and 'property tyrants',[48] and a curious American book of 1933 called *Apiatia: Little Essays on Honey-Makers* by Charles Waterman treats the drone-culling worker bees as Marxist revolutionaries:

> A leisure class always excites envy and jealousy with the less prosperous and the ostentation they often present inflames them to such an extent that a massacre ensues. The princes of Apiatia have always been subject to massacres. During the warm weather they have always been allowed to bask in the sunshine and partake of the ample supply of sustenance; but when winter comes, when sustenance must be measured by the number of mouths, then the unproductive must be sacrificed to the necessities of materialism; and jealousy sweetens the necessity, then the cry goes forth, 'Down with the princes. Death to princes. To those who produce belong the fruits.'[49]

Moffett's sixteenth-century economic view of the exclusion of the drones had been that shortage does cause rebellion within the hive, but that the drones are also eliminated to avoid unnecessary challenges to the king bee's authority which they foment in the form of popular sedition.[50] Waterman's inter-war bee fantasy in the same

Left: A French medal of the Second Republic (1848) by Eugène Oudiné.
Right: A 1794 coin from Geneva with a Republican beehive and the motto
travaille et economise.

vein inflects this theme with reference to events in Russia. The
argument is, however, somewhat compromised by daft vignettes of
bee life: he likes to think of the drones hankering after the queen
singing 'Only one girl in the world for me!' – far stranger than anything suggested by Virgil or Moffett.[51] Robert Graves invokes the
revolutionary drones rather differently in a poem of 1951: they are
complacent, seccessionary English Communists who fabricate a
'huge King bee to rule all hives forever'.[52] Henri Cole's 2004 poem
'The Lost Bee' invokes the ancient belief in the bee as the departing
soul in the desperate setting of a terrorist attack in some Middle
East battle zone: a bee, 'blood-sticky almsman', is bathing in a water
trough near a tangle of dead bodies recently gunned down. 'If
every man has a soul, these had fled or were fermenting.'[53] This
political bee, which seemed to be assuming some uneasy, discom-
fiting meanings in the Enlightenment and beyond, had in fact a
long tradition of moral ambivalence associated with its biology
and its behaviour.

five

Pious/Corrupt Bee

Wheras al other creatures (not bred of putrefaction) are subject
to libidinous heats in their kinds, the Bee is free thereof,
and multiplies by a way more chast.
H. Hawkins, *Parthenia Sacra* (1633)[1]

For Christian writers of the Middle Ages the political
wisdom of bees was indissoluble from other moral qualities. The emblem of holiness and innocence, the bee had
been the winged servant of God, and was the only creature to
escape the Garden of Eden before the consequences of Adam's
fall could be visited upon it with all the rest of creation. Some such
association of bees with the prelapsarian condition exists from
earliest times, and flourished throughout Europe and the Middle
East. In Hittite myth, Adam and Eve were accompanied by bees
as they fled Eden. Originally white, the bee of Hungarian myth
turned brown and narrow-waisted after fighting with Satan,
who caught her doing errands for God, the 'insect' or 'incised'
join of her thorax and the abdomen cut by the lash of his whip,
her stripes the mark of its lash (one of bee-kind's primary antag-
onists is the wasp, the devil's attempt to create a bee). A related
tradition identified her stripes as the scar of the flaming angelic
swords as the bee fled the Garden. In the Qu'ran, An-Nahl, the
bee, is told by Allah to go out into the world to make hives and
collect nectar so that the honey may be of use to mankind: 'There

comes from within it a beverage of many colours, in which there is healing for men.'[2]

Although in the classical Golden Age there was honey but no bees,[3] Welsh tradition concurred that bees originated in Paradise and left it because of man's sin. God blessed them, and mass was not to be said without beeswax candles. In Dante's *Paradiso* the mystic Rose of Paradise is flanked by a bee-like angel host.[4] Wordsworth recalls this tradition in the *Vernal Ode* when he observes:

> Humming Bee!
> Thy sting was needless then, perchance unknown,
> The seeds of malice were not sown;
> All creatures met in peace, from fierceness free,
> And no pride blended with their dignity.[5]

Bees were thought to be chaste: H. Hawkins doubted that bees had any kind of sexual differentiation among them, 'but if they have, they are Mayds, or Bachelours everie one, because they have no marriages with them, as living very chastly togeather like so manie Angels'.[6] The classical writers had fostered the idea of the virgin bee: Virgil, following Aristotle, claims that 'they gather children from the leaves and flow'rs'.[7] The tradition that bees reproduce asexually associated them with the cult of the Virgin, and they are very often seen in representations of her as a sign of her own spotlessness. Just as the Blessed Virgin lives on the heavenly dew of divine grace, so the bee 'feeds no worse then of the deaw, that falls from Heaven'.[8] By extension the bee became symbolic of 'the incomprehensible generation of the Sonne of God'.[9] Bees, honey, honeycomb and wax are all associated with purity: in the Christian tradition, as the Welsh custom suggests, beeswax candles were pure sources of light, unlike tallow candles which were tainted by fleshliness, and were required implements in the Roman rite. The wax represented the spotless flesh of Christ, the wick his soul and the flame the divinity which dominates both.[10] The Ukrainian folk-art *pysanky*, the vividly colourful decoration of eggs using vegetable dyes and beeswax, claims its origin from the decorated eggs which Mary offered to Pilate when she pleaded for her son's life; it is also said that a pedlar's basket of plain eggs for market was transformed into *pysanky* when he assisted Christ bearing his cross.

Bees and their products, always connected with civil virtue, are associated in Christian thought with its particular brand of self-sacrifice and with truth itself. The word of God is sometimes compared to honey in the mouth; and the Psalms exhort the Israelites to walk in the ways of God and thereby to be satisfied by Him with 'honey out of the rock'.[11] Bees and honey-making were nevertheless firmly yoked in the Gospel to the practicalities of living in the world: Christ chose to eat a piece of honeycomb to prove to his disciples that he had risen in body as well as in spirit.[12]

Thomas of Cantimpré, a thirteenth-century French Dominican monk, wrote of the life of bees as a model for the Christian clergy, the stingless 'king' bee the mild bishop, the lay-members of the monastic orders the drones. He also likens the foraging of bees to the scholarship of the great religious orders and their gathering of the sweet nectar of the ancients and of the Fathers of the Church.[13] A seventeenth-century Puritan writer on practical fruit-growing reconciled the busyness of bees with the Sabbatarian injunction to refrain from work on Sunday:

Our Eyes . . . ought as little Bees fall upon Severall objects and from them (as from so many Flowers) gather hony, and bring it into the hive; that is, sweet, heavenly, wholsome Meditations for magnifying the Creator in all his Attributes.[14]

The Virgin Mary discovered in a hive, from a late-13th-century Galician manuscript life of the Virgin.

Our Lady of Pilgrimage, from a painted hive of 1869.

Richard Rolle, the medieval homilist, noted that three aptitudes of bees stand for three virtues in the Christian man: the bee is never idle, it carries a little earth as ballast in its feet as it flies, and it keeps its wings bright. So wise men are never idle, they never forget their vile earthliness and they keep their charitable instincts in full play.[15] It was a conceit still being used by a Victorian poet who exhorted: 'With bee-like industry fill thou the hive/Of knowledge … Lay up rich fuel for poetic use …'.[16] A modern secular version of the medieval clerical bee is imagined by Rilke, who regards the poet's internalizing of the threatened phenomenal world as a foraging and conversion of the precious things of this world into an ineffable poetic substance to be laid up for nourishment: 'We are the bees of the invisible. We desperately plunder the honey of the visible to gather it into the great golden hive of the invisible.'[17]

A number of the church fathers – Ambrose, Augustine, Jerome, Basil and Tertullian – compared Christ's life to that of the bee: the bee brings forth its young through its mouth 'as Christe . . . proceeded from his Father's mouth'.[18] Others used the supposed virginity of bees as the emblem of cloistered religious and the flight of the bee as a symbol of the heaven-bound soul, a tradition possibly inherited from Pythagoras, who believed that in metempsychosis the souls of the wise and ingenious passed into the bodies of bees. Bees and eagles, according to widespread European folklore, are the only animals with access to heaven.[19] The Italian Emanuele Tesauro, quoting Virgil, noted that 'Esse Apibus partem Divinae Mentis, et hautus Aetherios dixere: ma i Filosofi Christiani furono stretti di confessare un Vestigio di ragione negli Animali inragionevoli.' [It is said that bees share divine intelligence by drinking ethereal draughts: but Christian philosophers were strict in admitting a remnant of reason in these irrational animals.][20]

A 17th-century woodcut linking bees and scholarship.

Dead bees could be resurrected, according to ancient writers like Columella and Varro, if their ashes were mixed with sweet wine and exposed to sunlight, and this was a tradition supported as late as the seventeenth century by Purchas and Moffett.[21] Indeed, belief in apian resurrection (perhaps mixed up with the competing legend of the corruptive origin of bees, who supposedly arose from dead carcasses) is probably one root of the whole range of theological traditions which associated bees with godliness, immortality, innocence and spirituality. Later writers, even when they had abandoned the notion of the virginal bee, believed in the bee's modesty ('whatsoever the Bees do in *Venus* service they act in secret, and far remove from the eyes and knowledge of all men');[22] and they linked the bee with their nostalgia for the golden age, when men and animals lived peacefully. It is possibly a remnant of this association of bees with virginity, innocence, and monastic seclusion that encouraged the twentieth-century monks of Buckfast Abbey in Devon, under Brother Adam, to extend the technologies of beekeeping, most notably in the development of the 'Buckfast' strain of high-producing, disease-resistant and famously gentle honeybees, now distributed worldwide.

The spiritual capacity of bees did not die away with the Reformation and the failure of the monastic orders in England. The following extraordinary anecdote of bees was reported as fact in 1609. An old countrywoman, according to Charles Butler, a Hampshire vicar and musicologist, found that her bees were suffering from a murrain plague. Her friend advised her to cure them by placing a fragment of the Host in the hive. This she did, and when some time later she opened the hive to check on the health of her bees she discovered that they were not only recovered but had built a chapel of wax, complete with a bell-tower and bells, and that they had placed the wafer on the wax altar and were buzzing in harmony around it.[23] That tale is retold by Robert Hawker in 1899 as 'a parable of sacred things' by which we are reminded that even 'mighty sages cannot see/ The deep foundations of the bee', and that the smallest and humblest parts of creation may 'fondly dream of mysteries divine'.[24] In Renaissance emblem books, bees were said to be *sine iniuria* ('harmless'), *operosa et sedula* ('active and diligent'), full of *candor ingenuus* ('perfect honesty'), and living signs that *omne tulit punctum* ('everything has a sting', from *omne tulit punctum, qui miscuit utile dulci* ('everything which mixes delight and use carries a sting')).[25]

Violence by humans against bees, however, always had moral weight: 'unjust custom' in human affairs was compared to the old practice of 'those cruell Bee-masters [who] burne the poore Athenian bees for their hony, or else drive them from the best part thereof by their long practiced cunninge'.[26] Sir Walter Raleigh characterized Henry VIII's mercilessness toward his nobles and minions in terms of destructive apiculture: 'To how many', he exclaimed, 'gave he abundant flowers from whence to gather honey, and in the end of harvest burnt them in the hive!'[27] Because 'they work for al, they watch for al, they fight for al',[28] the 'oeco-nomic' and political virtues of 'studious, industrious, laborious'[29] bees made acts against their innate and pious civility especially hein-ous. As symbols of justice, according to Solomon, 'civil and well nurtured Bees . . . will not refuse the care of the Bee-master who hath skill, but will much love and delight in it'.[30] Thus Moses Rusden deplores the practice of killing bees for their honey, 'that cruelty exercised on those poor industrious creatures . . . which is so like the method of the Devil, that paies his most industrious servants with the greatest ruine'.[31]

Bees were commonly destroyed with sulphur or other kinds of lethal smoke. James Boswell interested himself in the non-lethal

Industrious bees, with a sting in the tail: *Omne tulit punctum* ('Everything has a sting'); from Diego di Saavedra Fajardo, *Idea Principis* (1640).

honey harvesting which he observed in 1765 in a Corsican convent of Franciscan monks. The monks apparently used juniper wood, 'the smoak of which makes the bees retire ... They never kill a bee,' he notes with satisfaction.[32] The late-eighteenth-century diarist Anne Hughes was discomfited by the natural injustice of killing bees for honey. 'It do grieve me,' she wrote, 'to kill the poor things, being such a waste of good bees, to lie in a great heap at the bottom of the hole when the skep be took off it, but we do want the honey.'[33] William Cotton, the lively nineteenth-century English apiarist who sent the first honeybees to New Zealand, was a major voice in the 'Never Kill a Bee' movement, founded by Thomas Nutt in the 1830s. Cotton reports being told by a country

The privacy and modesty of apian existence is noted in the motto *Nulli patet* ('Not open to view'); from Diego di Saavedra Fajardo's *Idea Principis*.

bee-master that the ghosts of his burned bees always appeared to him the night after they died, and an old woman claimed that she would never omit to go to church on the Sunday following her bee-burning.[34] In recompense, Cotton assures the creatures themselves in a later book, 'the Bees of England will make much [profit] by me',[35] as country beekeepers learn by him to conserve their bees. A modern rendition of kindness and civility to bees is Diana Hartog's 'Polite to Bees', in which a woman who seems to grow wings of honey then wonders nervously if she 'might fly – without giving offence'.[36]

Not all writers, however, have been impressed by apian civility. Samuel Purchas notes that there are 'no greater robbers of Bees,

François Rudé,
*Aristaeus Mourning
the Loss of his Bees*,
1830, bronze.

than bees', and points out that our expectation that these sociable creatures should 'converse one with another in love and peace' is unreasonable: 'they fight not then for their right, but to get a booty, and under the colour of warring, make a trade of robbing'. Indeed, he says, bees often rob other bees for fun.[37] Joseph Hall, Bishop of Norwich in the seventeenth century, moralized the battles of bees:

> What a pitty it is to see these profitable, industrious Creatures fall so furiously upon each other, and thus sting and kill each other, in the very mouth of the Hive; I could like well to see the Bees doe this execution upon Waspes and droanes, enemies to their common stocke, this savours but of Justice; But to see them fall foule upon those of their owne wing, it cannot but trouble the owner, who must needs be an equall leeser by the victory of either.[38]

A. I. Root, the nineteenth-century doyen of American beekeeping whose publishing company produced *Apiatia*, wrote rather cynically about the greed of bees:

> With all of their wonderful instincts, I have never been able to gather that the bees of one hive ever have any spark of solicitude as to the welfare of their neighbors. If, by the loss of a queen, the population of any hive becomes weak, and the bees too old to defend their stores, the very moment the fact is discovered by other colonies they rush in and knock down the sentinels, with the most perfect indifference, plunder the ruined home of its last bit of provision, and then rejoice in their own home, it may be but a yard away, while their defrauded neighbors are so weak from starvation as to have fallen to the bottom of the hives, being only just able to attempt feebly to crawl out at the entrance. Had it been some of their own flock, the case would have been very different indeed; for the first bee of a starving colony will carry food around to its comrades, as soon as it has imbibed enough of the food furnished to have the strength to stagger to them.[39]

For all their history of civility, piety, and innocence, bees have another tradition attached to them: if on the one hand bees were virginal and innocent, on the other they were understood by the naturalists to be 'imperfect', that is, their generation was thought to be corruptive because, in several traditions, they hatched from rotting carcasses, and 'equivocal' because their parturition was abnormal, the larval forms being entirely unlike the mature parents. This curious tradition originated with the Egyptians, and is present in the earliest Greek writers: bees are born from rotting matter. The Egyptians said that the bee arose from Apis, the sacred

'Out of the strong came forth sweetness' (Judges 14:5–14).

bull of Egypt and embodiment of Osiris, god of resurrection. A buried bull (or one suffocated and shut in a sealed room) was thought to engender new bees, a belief almost certainly derived in explanation of the apparently miraculous phenomenon of abiogenesis, the emergence of creatures from mud observed in the Nile Delta. The tradition turns up in the Old Testament, when Samson kills a young lion with his bare hands and finds a swarm of bees and their honey in the carcass, from which he generated the riddle 'Out of the eater came forth meat, and out of the strong came forth sweetness.'[40] The tradition was handed on to the Greeks, who adopted apis as the word for bee, and adapted by the Greek and later the Roman writers: according to Virgil, the hero Aristaeus who pursued Eurydice and accidentally caused her death was punished by the death of all his bees.[41] He was then advised by Proteus to sacrifice cattle in placation, and nine days after the sacrifice he found new swarms of bees in the carcasses. Ovid includes this story of the ox-born bee in *Metamorphoses*.[42] Bees 'born' from specific animals produced a hierarchy of honeys, the noblest bees emerging from the noblest animals, and lion-, calf- and ox-honey thought to be the best kinds. Apicultural writers until the late-seventeenth century regularly advised their readers to set the carcass of a calf near their hives to encourage the procreation of the best honeymakers. Aristotle described this phenomenon: 'If . . . they breed not, but fetch their young elsewhere, of necessity it must bee, that there be Bees without any labour of Bees, namely in that place from whence they fetch their seed; for why do they come to perfection, being carried away, and not in their own proper places?'[43] This ability to reproduce without copulation he attributes to 'a defect of Nature's bounty towards them, because otherwise *nihil ut apum, habent genus divinitatis*' ('no creatures have the stamp of divinity except the bee').[44] This tradition arose out of the confusion surrounding all insects, who – except for the bee and a few other social insects, as it turns out – lay eggs which they immediately abandon. And in the case of bees, the confusion was probably compounded by their likeness to hoverflies, which do indeed lay their eggs in putrid matter. The queen bee, of course, only lays in the wax cells of the hive. The observed presence of maggots and other insect larvae in putrid matter was thought to be a sign of the innate corruption of all creatures under heaven: we are all tending toward decay, and it is at death that the decadent elements in our very bodies become visible and obvious. Thus bees were described as 'mixt imperfect creatures' which are *generantur ex putri* ... engendred of corruption'.[45] Without good microscopes, no one could detect that mature insects (though not bees) were simply laying their eggs in promising sources of larval nutrition, and the tradition of corruptive reproduction persisted into the late-seventeenth century.[46] In 1705 Maria Merian presented a South American bee with its spawn apparently in the form of foam on a branch (actually the eggs of the tent-caterpillar), a phenomenon still known as 'bee-spit'.

Although the young William Cotton tried to reproduce bees in this way after reading Hartlib on the subject, the idea had long since died out as a serious scientific premiss by the late-eighteenth century. It retained an attractive metaphoric power, however, which surfaces in Wordsworth's 'Vernal Ode', and in a Whittier poem of the late 1860s. Although 'dead seemed the legend', 'The Hive at Gettysburg' invokes the biblical story of Samson and the honey-filled lion to meditate on a beehive constructed in a Confederate Army drum abandoned on the battlefield during the American Civil War:

> ... A stained and shattered drum
> Is now the hive where, on their flowery rounds,
> The wild bees go and come.
>
> Unchallenged by a ghostly sentinel,
> They wander wide and far,
> Along green hillsides, sown with shot and shell,
> Through vales once choked with war.
> The low reveille of their battle-drum
> Disturbs no morning prayer;

Aristaeus discovering bees in his dead cattle, from Virgil's *Georgics* as illustrated by Wencelaus Hollar.

With deeper peace in summer noons their hum
Fills all the drowsy air.
And Samson's riddle is our own to-day,
Of sweetness from the strong,
Of union, peace, and freedom plucked away
From the rent jaws of wrong.

Maria Merian's illustration of a South American bee and its supposed egg-mass on a leaf of a 'tabrouba' tree; from Maria Sibylla Merian's *Metamorphoses Insectorum Surinamensis* (1705).

From Treason's death we draw a purer life,
As, from the beast he slew,
A sweetness sweeter for his bitter strife
The old-time athlete drew![47]

The honey made by the bees is culled from a landscape seemingly sprouting bullets for vegetation; the drum, like the lion in the Bible, is a defeated enemy from whom the reward of victory is 'a purer life' of 'union, peace, and freedom'. The Gettysburg Address haunts the background of this poem: like Lincoln's heroic vow of devotion at this same battlefield, Whittier's vision of ultimate sweetness out of a terrifying and horrific struggle is converted with the epic simile of the 'old-time athlete' into an equally heroic vignette, the bees in the drum clearly linked to the emblem *ex bello pax*, bees in a derelict helmet. And yet the landscape's bittersweet ambience of the unconcerned insects wandering the hillsides as if nothing cataclysmic had ever happened there argues against Lincoln at Gettysburg: the world *can* forget what brave men did here. Nations will rise and fall, armies will be slaughtered, but in the end bees – Union, Confederate and even Middle Eastern bees, like those of Henri Cole's poem – will go out to seek nectar and nature will prevail over memory. It is bees, even more than men, who will give the last full measure of devotion to their nation, a nation which, unlike the Confederacy and the Union, will not perish from the earth.

Bees, it was said, had been excluded along with most other insects from Noah's Ark because of their corruptive imperfection. The predicament of the unworthy or fallen bee and the undoubted industry and utility of its honey-making yielded an interesting apian paradox: precisely because of its imperfection, the creature achieves virtue through its hard work and altruism. This provided an instructive hint to mankind: like fallen man, the bee had to suffer the consequences of its imperfection; and, like the bee, man could repair the damage by virtue of hard work. The amendment of the Adamic lapse in man was particularly connected to bees in late-eighteenth-century America, with its pronounced reverence for providential success and a stern work ethic. There, the slang term 'bee' indicated any social gathering devised to perform some concerted beneficial task (the quilting bee, the husking bee, the barnraising bee, the spelling bee and so on), and persists today.

The principle of apian cooperation (*non nobis*) is a political one, but it is founded in use and benefit, in the best interests of all. But of what use are bees to us?

six

Utile Bee

Well then, let this be your first rule, Never kill one.
William Cotton, *A Short and Simple Letter to Cottagers,*
from a Conservative Bee-Keeper (1838)[1]

Invited by the BBC's *Desert Island Discs* programme to imagine the single luxury he would most like to have as an island castaway, Suggs – the eminently sane lead singer of the 1980s band Madness – chose a beehive. A hive would, Suggs explained, give him honey for energy, beeswax for candles and skin protection, and royal jelly as a nutritional supplement; in addition, he would derive comfort and philosophical pleasure in his solitude by contemplating the life of bees.[2] The bee, it seems, is still admired for the material and moral profit it confers on mankind. But what exactly does this profit amount to?

A recent estimate of the economic value of honey suggests that the current cost of the mortality rate from cancer in the United States would be substantially reduced with the development of honey's known and suspected anti-carcinogenic properties, not to mention the low cost of honey as a medicine compared to prescription drugs which treat many of the other ailments honey can alleviate.[3] The medicinal properties of honey have sometimes been disputed by conventional medicine, which regards them as meaningless folk remedies, but there is now conclusive evidence that it is a powerful specific against a number of ailments. Both Pythagoras (sixth century BC), and Democritus (fifth century BC) attributed their long lives to the consumption of honey, but its medicinal profit was recognized at least 5,000 years ago. A Sumerian tablet of 3000 BC recommends it for skin ulcers; honey-butter was used in the Ayurvedic surgery of ancient India as a topical dressing, and similar uses for honey were known in ancient Egypt and Greece.

Nor has it lost its place in our pharmacopoeia. It is used against burns and wounds of many kinds. The Bulgarian army during the Balkan War of 1913, having run short of medical supplies, dressed wounds with honey. The sticky liquidity of honey makes it the ideal medium for wound and burn dressings because it does not solidify and tear the healing flesh when the dressings are changed. One of the enzymes added by bees to nectar in the honey sac is glucose oxidase; this reacts with the glucose in the nectar to make gluconic acid, which lowers the pH of honey and increases its acidity, inhibiting bacterial growth and allowing it to resist fermentation so that it can be stored for long periods. A by-product of gluconic acid is the microbicide hydrogen peroxide. The combination, therefore, of low moisture, low pH and hydrogen peroxide (H_2O_2) makes honey an effective antiseptic agent, and it is a specific against, among others, the bacteria which cause anthrax, diphtheria, septicæmia, various urinary tract infections, impetigo, tooth decay, puerperal fever, scarlet fever and cholera.[4] Very recently, honey has been shown to be specific also against *Helicobacter pylori*, the agent implicated in stomach cancer, because it stimulates the production of stomach peptides and increases blood-flow to the stomach lining. It has also been licensed for use in the National Health Service, and is known to be effective against MRSA, the super-bug, an increasingly common hospital-borne infection which resists most antibiotics, and against the staph infections which are common in hospitals and have also become increasingly resistant. Moreover, the hydrogen

Worker bees fill honey-cells.

peroxide in honey is released slowly by being suspended in a viscous solution, so that it is more effective over the healing period than the straight application of undiluted H_2O_2.[5]

After it is regurgitated out of the honey sac, the nectar's transformation into honey is continued in the hive, where the bees evaporate its moisture and it becomes a supersaturated solution with high osmolarity – the ability to draw off water, in this case from bacterial and fungal cells, thus dehydrating them. Again, this property has evolved to kill the enemies of stored honey, but it is a feature which further assists in the curative and healing process of honey on wounds and in infections. Honey is also high in flavonoids, which are able to penetrate the lens of the eye. Aristotle and the ancient Maya both knew that honey could relieve eye inflammations and cataracts. It is for this reason that human corneas for transplant are packed in honey. Some claims have been made for honey as an antioxidant, and as an enhancer of the immune system (it allegedly stimulates the multiplication of B- and T-lymphocytes). These claims have not been verified and require more investigation.[6] Honey is still used very widely in internal medicines, especially in cough remedies and for mouth ulcers. Its effectiveness in these cases is as likely to be the result of its viscous and soothing texture as of any strictly pharmacological or antibacterial agency. It appears, too, that propolis, the plant resin used by bees in nest-repair, has its own antibacterial properties which make it effective against dental decay. Royal jelly, however, the glandular secretion given as food by workers to larvae which are to be raised as queens in the hive, although many claims have been made for it as an expensive human food supplement, has no obvious benefits.

Samuel Hartlib estimated in the 1650s that £300,000 was the gross national profit in England from honey and beeswax – a fortune by the reckoning of the time, but a figure which might have seemed low to John Aubrey somewhat later in the century. That indefatigable collector of interesting miscellaneous facts tells us that Charles Butler, the author of *The Feminine Monarchie*, gave his daughter a handsome dowry of £400 in honey ('he call'd her his Honey-girle'), that bees belonging to a Wiltshire neighbour of his produced half a pound of honey a day, and that a Newcastle beekeeper he had heard of was earning £800 per annum (a superb income), all of which give an indication of how valuable a commodity honey could be in this period.[7] Among the many enthusiastic seventeenth-century promoters of apian industries, his contemporary John Levett reminded his readers of the use of bee products in domestic hygiene, physick and surgery, all presented as a dialogue between a beekeeper and his attentive student. Hartlib's *The Reformed Commonwealth of Bees* (1655) reprints bee-enquiries and discussions which have been sent to him by various correspondents, a prototype of the modern *Beekeepers' Journal*. In the twentieth century, the propriety of beekeeping as a 'life skill' was being touted by Thornton College in Buckinghamshire, a convent-run school for girls whose 1943 advertisement offered it among its 'homecrafts' to pupils not preparing for examinations or for university;[8] it may have been an especially attractive accomplishment during the period of wartime shortages.

Since Aristotle, Varro and Columella, writers had concentrated on the practical and profitable aspects of apiculture, and this continued into the industrial period. A Victorian 'cyclopaedia' of beekeeping offers a lengthy entry under 'profits in bees' which includes a number of cautionary anecdotes about managing the business for maximum returns, and advocates good modern apiculture – medicating rather than killing the bees at harvest time, preserving the combs during honey-extraction rather than destroying them. A moderate hive of about 80,000 bees, with three supers, the article assures its readers, can expect to yield 150 lbs (68 kg) of honey in a good year.[9] Fanciful beehives made by one John Milton were displayed at the Great Exhibition, including one shaped like a multi-family town house and containing four separate hives, like flats, a gimmick designed to show that even urban dwellers could expect profit from bees, and reminding spectators of the creature's harmonious tendencies and hard work.[10]

Aside from the use of beeswax in candles and the numerous medical uses of honey, bee products are surprisingly versatile. Beeswax, having an unusually high melting-point (145°F/63°C), a very high burning-point (2,100°F/1,149°C), as well as great strength, is used in modelling and casting, polishes and coatings, lubricants, electrical transducers, and pharmaceuticals and cosmetics.

Bee 'product' includes essential drinks of an earlier period, when wine was an expensive import and drinking water was potentially tainted. The working- and middle-classes in England and northern

Europe would have made and consumed mead (probably the oldest manufactured human drink), a kind of fermented honey wine or honey beer; metheglin or spiced mead; pyment, a concoction of fermented grape-juice and honey (particularly favoured by the Elizabethans); melomel, a fruit and honey wine; cyser, a honeyed cider; braggot, made of honey and malt sugars; and hippocras, a herbally enhanced grape and honey wine. The word 'honeymoon' itself derives from the old Germanic practice of drinking mead or honey ale at weddings, and it could be quite powerful stuff: the British army during the Napoleonic wars was given mead ale for a time, but it was found to be too strong for the soldiers at 6 per cent alcohol.[11]

One third of the total human diet derives from insect-pollinated plants, and the health of the bee population is an important indicator of certain aspects of wider ecological health. The image of the working bee as poster animal for the organic and green movements and for various nature conservancy initiatives in America and Europe is a familiar one. Thoreau frequently alludes in his journals to the presence of bees and their foods in various regions of New England, as do the American frontiersmen, who read the presence of wild bees as a providential sign of an abundant wilderness already in the process of redemption by civil insects. William Cullen Bryant, in his important poem *The Prairies* (1836), describes the huge Midwestern landscape as a 'great solitude quick with life', where

> The bee,
> A more adventurous colonist than man,
> With whom he came across the eastern deep,
> Fills the savannas with his murmurrings,
> And hides his sweets, as in the golden age,
> Within the hollow oak. I listen long

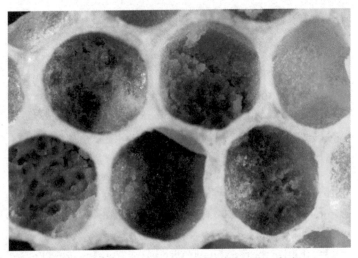

Pollen of different colours is stored in pollen cells in the hive.

To his domestic hum, and think I hear
The sound of that advancing multitude
Which soon shall fill these deserts.[12]

Bryant's frontier bees have an equivocal status in the poem – they are the intrepid outriders for the heroic national expansion to follow, and thus emblematic of manifest destiny; and yet their arrival signals to Bryant the effacement of 'that great solitude' and the ancient native societies within it which he celebrates in other poems with unusual feeling and sympathy. The bee, ever the bearer of multiple meanings, expresses the latent American uneasiness about the costs of the inevitable westward course of empire. By a gloomier providential logic, the failure of wild bee populations in the industrialized world is widespread, and the reduced vigour of bees signals a potential catastrophe in which earthly fertility would be ruined or deeply compromised.

seven

Aesthetic Bee

A worke of arte; and yet no arte of man,
Can worke, this worke, these little creatures can.
Geoffrey Whitney, *A Choice of Emblems* (1586)[1]

'There is one masterpiece, the hexagonal cell, that touches perfection. No living creature, not even man, has achieved, in the centre of his sphere, what the bee has achieved in her own; and were some one from another world to descend and ask of the earth the most perfect creation of the logic of life, we should needs have to offer the humble comb of honey.'[2] In the history of ideas there has always been something especially virtuous and admirable about beautiful utility – that is, not merely good practical and pleasing design, but rather the indivisible moral union of the aesthetic and the pragmatic. The legendary inventor and craftsman Daedalus, maker of the Cretan labyrinth, produced many practical items – the saw and the axe, for example – as well as extraordinary and wonderful things which alluded to pragmatic beauty. One of his most celebrated works was a golden honeycomb for the temple of Aphrodite on Mount Eryx. The honeycomb with its hexagonal cells is a needful beauty 'in whom all busy offices unite / With all fine functions that afford delight',[3] a structure perfectly pleasing because it is the most elegant solution to perfect functionality. Such structures have usually been judged the highest and most ethical form of creative act, and symbolically resemble paradisial structures.[4] Just as Andrew Marvell could praise a house for fitting the sensibility of its noble owner the way a tortoiseshell fits a tortoise, the honeycomb and the waxen cell is 'fit' for the worthy tasks of the bee. Thomas Browne studied the 'sexangular cels' as a sign or portent from God that 'nature geometrizeth': 'The edificial Palaces of Bees and Monarchical spirits' are full of wonder, he says: their six-cornered apartments 'declin[e] a circle, whereof many stand not close together, and compleatly fill the area of the place; But rather affecting a six-sided figure, whereof every cell affords a common side unto six more, and also a fit receptacle for the Bee itself '.[5] That the Enlightenment French naturalist René Réaumur considered basing the fixed measurement for his proposed decimal system on the hexagonal wax cell is no more than an extension of this sense of apian architecture as somehow perfect and divine.[6] Christopher Smart mocks a 'busy prattling blockhead' who dares recommend to a queen bee various improvements in apian architecture:

Ma'm, architecture you're not skill'd in,
I don't approve your way of building;
In this there's nothing like design.
Pray learn the use of *Gunter's* line.[7]

The twentieth-century novelist and sculptor Michael Ayrton used the figure of Daedalus to represent, as Joyce did, the sensibility of the enquiring and adventurous artist; like that mythic forebear, Ayrton made a golden honeycomb with gold bees on it using the lost wax method: the gorgeous artefact was inspired by bees and made by a technique requiring the product of bees.

There were a number of ideas about the method by which bees construct their combs, including some incorrect speculation by so

Two examples of the sculptor Michael Ayrton's 1968 golden honeycombs; that on the right stood for a time in the garden of Sir Edmund Hillary in New Zealand; real bees made use of this replica comb.

distinguished a naturalist as Agassiz. Amos Root took everyone to task when he discussed the practicality and the mathematics of the honeycomb in 1891. For tensile strength and efficiency of storage (both of larvae and of honey), the hexagonal cell is unsurpassed as a solution to a number of ergonomic and engineering problems. 'The construction of the bee-cell', says Root, 'became a famous problem in the economy of nature. *Take the money and buy a hive of bees*, all ye who thirst for knowledge, and take it direct from God's own works, instead of receiving it second hand.'[8] 'This hive', wrote Henry Ellison, as he compared the structure of his sonnet to a honeycomb, 'poetical hexagonal, is built in cells all equal, regular, and like, as those of the real beehive are; for strength, convenience, best form of all.'[9] In this and other poems, Ellison makes a bee triad, where bee foraging is likened to the getting of knowledge, the accumulation of experience, and the making of poetry.

The bee – its products, its behaviour, its body – appears everywhere in architecture, art and music but, as Karl Marx reminds us, the gulf between the bee and the artist touches the nature of creation:

by the complexity of its wax cells the bee puts more than one architect to shame. But from the outset, what differentiates the worst architect from the most expert bee is that he has built the cell in his head before building it in the hive.[10]

The most thoroughgoing example of apian-inspired architecture is that of the Catalan Antonio Gaudí, who incorporated features of bees, their hives, and of apicultural practices into his structural and decorative motifs. The rustic, skep-shaped beehives of his native Catalonia and the hanging architecture of the naturally produced wild honeycomb prompted his admiration for the parabolic arch, in particular. This appears over and over in his major works.[11] The civil life of the bee was another source of inspiration for Gaudí. His design (c. 1876) for the Cooperativa Obrera (Workers' Cooperative) at Mataró draws on Utopian ideas of the hive and on socialist principles of the solidarity of labour. Gaudí's design

Left: Gaudí's hive-inspired cupola in the Palacio Güell, Barcelona.
Right: The parabolic arches in Gaudí's Casa Battló, Barcelona, resemble the natural curve of a hanging honeycomb, inverted.

Left: Hanging combs in the wild, from L. L. Langstroth's *The Hive and the Honey-Bee* (1853).

Right: The municipal escutcheon of Le Chaux-de-Fonds, Switzerland.

for the Cooperativa's symbol was a bee – a choice made simultaneously in Le Chaux-de-Fonds in Switzerland, where one of the great watchmaking cooperatives was known as 'The Republic of the Bees' and whose factory interior was decorated with bee-related motifs. This Swiss town, with an ancient watchmaking and republican tradition, sports a beehive on its municipal escutcheon and is the birthplace of another bee-inspired architectural master, Edward Jeanneret, 'Le Corbusier'. Like many avant-garde artists of his time, he was especially interested by the work of entomologist Jean-Henri Fabre and by the behaviour and artefacts of the social insects, which show us that order is a natural phenomenon. Even Le Corbusier's least organically shaped buildings refer to the hive and the comb.[12] Peter Behrens's logo for the AEG company of Berlin extended the industrial affinity of the bee.

The hexagonal patterns of the sixteenth-century Alhambra palace at Granada and the beehive shapes of Gaudí's Barcelona Cathedral indicate the enduring appeal of the ingeniously fashioned honeycombs. Perhaps the most extravagant and elaborate extension of apian craft in modern art is to be found in the work of Joseph Beuys. In the late 1940s and early 1950s Beuys produced a number of sculptures in beeswax of the queen bee. Strongly influenced by Rudolf Steiner, Beuys wanted to represent the connection between physical and spiritual production. The queen bee series was a first attempt to indicate the principles of 'cooperation and brotherhood';[13] but the products of the bee – honey and wax – became even more significant for his 1965 performance piece, *How to Explain Pictures to a Dead Hare*, for which the artist anointed himself with honey and gold, and for the 1977 installation *Honey Pump at the Workplace*, a large hydraulic system which moved two tons of honey through clear tubes installed around the lecture hall of the Museum Fridericianum in Kassel. With the *Honey Pump* Beuys created an organic system in which honey represented the bloodstream of a social organization, as it is, in a sense, in the hive itself.

The development of rational and organic architectural responses to the bee in the late Victorian industrial period through the

Left: A dome in the Alhambra Palace, Granada, Spain.
Right: Hanging bees forming a parabolic arc over the comb; from Gilles-Augustin de Bazin, *Histoire Naturelle des Abeilles* (1744).

AEG's honeycomb
logo.

Modernist movement of the pre- and inter-war era did not deter
the more sentimental admirers of the bee. Maeterlinck's illustrator
Detmold persists with gauzy, dreamy scenes of bees and flowers;
Cecily Mary Barker's Edwardian flower fairies include a fat and
fuzzy 'busy old bumble bee' who contends with the Snapdragon
Elf for nectar; and Beatrix Potter's Babbitty Bumble and his apian
friends upset the precise housekeeping of Mrs Tittlemouse. Later
bee icons are purely frivolous or outrageous, such as the beehive
hairdos of the 1960s. Hive-shaped honeypots are probably the
most common example of bee kitsch; and bees advertise everything
from credit cards to spectacles to public sector financing.

In 1953 a German ethologist proposed that bees dance. The
means by which bees navigate their way to and from their food
sources – often remote from the hive – had never been fully understood, although the existence of the 'beeline', the straight flight
characteristic of laden bees returning to the hive with nectar and
pollen, had long been observed. This navigational ability is based
partly on physical landmarks which the bee can see with its compound eyes and partly on directional sensitivity to the earth's
magnetic field and to the position of the sun. Indeed, the sun is
probably key: starlight is almost certainly too faint for bees to per-
ceive, which is why even in warm weather they retire at night.
Nevertheless, before 1953 the secrets of how bees know where
they are were gradually being exposed.

Edward Detmold's romantic bee illustrating the 1924 edition of
Maeterlinck's *The Life of the Bee*.

What Karl von Frisch found was the answer to a more mysterious problem: how do bees communicate to each other what they know? A bee which has discovered a new source of food has some way of telling about it and of explaining its location to other bees without actually leading them to it. By the same token, when a

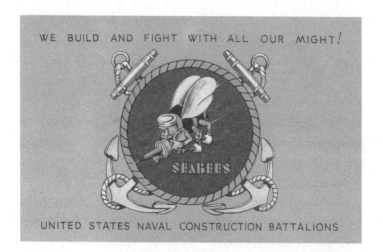

WE BUILD AND FIGHT WITH ALL OUR MIGHT!

SEABEES

UNITED STATES NAVAL CONSTRUCTION BATTALIONS

The emblem of the Fighting SeaBees, the Navy construction unit, in a World War II postcard.

The beehive hair-do as retro-chic in the hands of singer Mari Wilson, 1982.

swarm is looking for a new home, a scout bee is able to return from her expedition and deliver instructions about the site she has chosen, with instructions precise enough that the swarm can make its way there without further guidance. Von Frisch performed a series of controlled experiments with bees newly returned to the hive having found new food. He observed that these bees enacted one of two dances on the surface of the comb – the 'round dance' and the 'waggling dance' – and that these hive dances are a form of communication.

The round dance is used to announce the presence of food located near the hive. The flower scent which clings to the dancing bee helps the other bees to identify the flower they will be looking for and the vigour of the dance itself is probably related to the sweetness of the nectar. The round dance and waggling dance are both accompanied by a characteristic raising of the tip of the dancing bee's abdomen where the Nasinov gland releases a pheromone

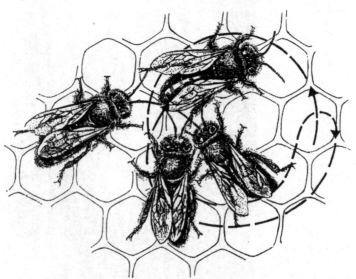

The round dance as described by Karl von Frisch.

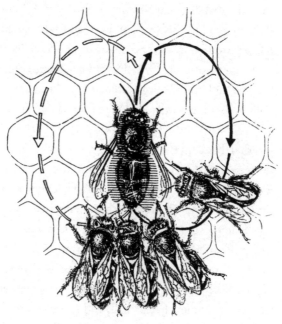

Von Frisch's waggling (or wagtail) dance.

announcing the presence of new food. The waggling dance is more complex, since it delivers information about food up to two or three miles away from the hive and must convey to other bees where to go without the aid of a scent trail. In this dance, variation in the speed of movement communicates distance, and the pattern of the dance probably gives directional instructions either by reference to gravity or to the position of the sun. Because bees on a mission to get or deliver food will fly in the straight 'beeline' if possible, and at steady elevation, the directions given in the waggling dance do not appear to account for detours around or over obstacles such as hills and buildings, and von Frisch concludes that there is no word for 'up' in bee language. The danced instructions eliminate any manoeuvres out of the beeline, so that bees know, as it were, the coordinates of where they are going to get food rather than the details of the journey itself.[14] Von Frisch won a Nobel Prize in 1973 for his work on bees, and subsequent research has refined the description and explanation of each dance.

The scientific confirmation of bee dances chimes with much bee-lore and much sentimentalizing of the creature, often (especially in the nineteenth century) portrayed as a happy-go-lucky little fella enjoying himself in capers and japes in sunny gardens. But whether 'bee dance' is a charming misnomer or not, bees really do seem to sing. The variations in pitch produced by the irregular flight of a foraging worker bee – that 'slender sound' and 'faint utterance' which Wordsworth remembered had accompanied 'ages coming, ages gone', the sound of summer days which William Cullen Bryant imagined as a murmuring wind, and Emerson as a 'mellow breezy bass'[15] – is reproduced by Rimsky-Korsakov's famous 'The Flight of the Bumble-Bee', a work about an aristocrat who can become a bee at will, and sounds and even looks like the creature's foraging flight among the flowers.

The weaving flight of Rimsky-Korsakov's 1900 'Flight of the Bumble-Bee'.

The nineteenth century was especially attracted to bee-music – there are at least four 'bee glees' from 1811 onwards[16] – and it is unsurprising that even the robustly active Walt Whitman could pause to contemplate the music of bumble bees 'humming their perpetual rich mellow boom'. He asked himself 'is there not a hint in it for a musical composition, of which it should be the background? Some bumble-bee symphony?'[17] As if in response, the Rimsky-Korsakov has recently been orchestrated for a symphony of pre-recorded bee-buzzes. The singing of bees was discussed in 1609 by Charles Butler, who rendered bee voices as follows:

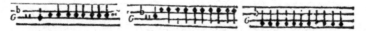

Bee voices, from Charles Butler, *The Feminine Monarchie* (1609).
From left to right: the new queen; the new queen in alarm; the old queen.

Butler also composed a madrigal about bees ('As of all states the Monarchie is best, So of all Monarchies that Feminine, of famous Amazons excels the rest');[18] the parts for this madrigal, following standard practice in the period, are laid out four-square on the page so that the four singers seated around a table can all read from the same sheet, an unmeant little musical emblem of the cooperative bee nation. The bee's wings, beating at more than two hundred times per second, produce an intense hum, and this 'voice' of the bee was imagined as almost choral in earlier times, with hives apparently celebrating the birth of Christ on Christmas morning or dirging their dead keepers. The work of Edward Farrington Woods, the beekeeping BBC sound-engineer who invented the apidictor, established that the workers and the drones have different wing-beat frequencies, and hum at 250 HZ (or B below middle C) and 190 HZ (or flattish G below middle C) respectively.[19]

The long tradition of the socially organized bee yielded up a subject to another composer, John Dowland, who, unlike Rimsky-Korsakov, did not attempt to reproduce the sound of bees. The lyrics of his madrigal 'It was the time when silly bees could speak' are reputedly by the Earl of Essex, who casts himself as a supplicant bee who, in spite of his hard labour, has failed to gain preferment when even drones, wasps, worms, gnats and butterflies all gorge on the thyme honey he helps to produce.

> Mated with grief, I kneeled on my knees,
> And thus complain'd unto the King of Bees.

'My liege, gods grant thy time may never end,
And yet vouchsafe to hear my plaint of thyme,
Which fruitless flies have found to have a friend,
And I cast down when atomies do climb.'

The King replied but thus, 'Peace, peevish bee,
Thou'rt bound to serve the time, the thyme not thee.'[20]

Essex's image of the king bee is ironically mistaken: the sovereign
to whom he was complaining was, of course, Elizabeth I. In 1602,
with the failure of his rebellion and his arraignment for treason,
Essex's play on unfavouring time would have been all too literal.

eight

Folkloric Bee

The tradition of the fabulous origin of bees . . .
I would rather attribute to poetic license than
submit to the test of our belief.
Columella, *De Rustica*[1]

Commonplaces about bees are so numerous that they have infiltrated our thinking about ourselves. Shakespeare is a good index of such apian conceits, ideas he uses, it seems, almost conventionally to express complex ideas of justice, virtue, policy and vengeance. Virtually all Shakespeare's bee references occur in the histories or the political tragedies, plays in which civil order of one kind or another is a primary theme. Mobs, for example, are likened to enraged and disorderly bees who 'care not who they sting' in *Henry VI, Part 2* (III.ii, 125–7); in *Titus Andronicus* they are like a crowd too willing to be urged by their leader to vengeance (V.i, 13–16). Base men are like the lazy and cowardly drones who 'suck not eagles' blood but rob beehives' (*Henry VI, Part 2*, IV.i, 107–10). This arises from an old belief that drones, as the food of eagles, in return go to eagles' nests and push the eggs out or suck them dry.[2] The natural nobility of bees is warped by Shakespeare into the practice of petty vengeance and also into internecine strife between bee and bee.

In *Henry VI, Part 1*, Talbot's complex imagery of uncertainty in the battle against Joan of Arc invokes directionless swarms:

A witch by fear, not force, like Hannibal
Drives back our troops and conquers as she lists.
So bees with smoke and doves with noisome stench
Are from their hives and houses driven away. (I.v, 19–24)

Joan of Arc's martial symbol was a beehive, and witches were sometimes accused of taking bee form in medieval Scottish legend. Talbot's bee image works both positively as a sympathetic representation of his valiant but overmastered army, and negatively as evilly possessed creatures in the toils of La Pucelle's sorcery. These images are troublingly equivocal: the scattered and bested English bees are defeated by an adversary who is the victorious 'queen' bee.

Shakespeare's second group of history plays develops some of its most important ideas of self-governance through the example of the bee. When Warwick tries to assure Henry IV that his apparently wastrel son Prince Hal will eventually mend his ways by 'turning past evil to advantages', the pessimistic and disillusioned father replies that such an outcome '[is] doubtful when the bee doth leave her comb/ in the dead carrion' (*Henry IV, Part 2*, IV.i, 79–80). The bee which has made its nest and produced honey in a carcass – a reference to the ox-born bee and the honey-filled lion killed by Samson – will rarely abandon it. By the same reasoning, Hal is not likely to forego his pleasures in the corrupt society where he has established them. The apian metaphor is extended further. *Henry V* (the reformed Hal now king) will, as we know, later use the civil emblem of the bee to describe his reign, but his father's despairing character of his son at a moment when he himself is beset by civil war and rebellion links the familial, the internecine and the chaotic: both filial relations and the civil hierarchy look to him like a debased beehive. Henry talks of the careful raising of sons by fathers:

For this they have engrossed and pilèd up
The cankered heaps of strange-achievèd gold;
For this they have been thoughtful to invest
Their sons with arts and martial exercises.
When like the bee tolling from every flower
[The virtuous sweets,]
Our thighs packed with wax, our mouths with honey,
We bring it to the hive, and like the bees,
Are murdered for our pains. This bitter taste
Yields his engrossments to the ending father. (IV.v, 70–79)

The virtue of bees is inverted as greed, envy and bitterness: the 'strange-achievèd gold' emerges as 'cankered' honey whose virtuous sweetness is ultimately of 'bitter taste'. The fabled foresight of bees in training their young and their selflessness in producing wax and honey is spurned here by those ungrateful sons who appropriate these goods wantonly. Shakespeare seems to be mingling the sloth of the male drones and the enmity of 'injurious wasps [who] feed on such sweet honey,/ And kill the bees which yield it' (*Two Gentlemen of Verona*, I.ii, 107–8).

Many superstitions connect the civil life of bees to human social and spiritual functions. For example, bees are celebrated nurturers: the gods Pan and Dionysus were bee-fed; and Zeus was fed by bees when his mother Rhea hid him in a cave in Mount Dicte to keep him safe from his murderous father Kronos. For this reason Zeus was sometimes styled *melissaios*, or 'bee-man'. He later rewarded the bees by giving them their stings to use against mankind, but by decreeing also that any bee who stings dies he enforced *non nobis* as a natural law. In some versions of the myth the protecting bees were actually women – the *melissae*, the daughters of King Melisseus. The priestesses in the temples of Cybele, Artemis and

An Etruscan vase showing Cretan honey-hunters stung by bees.

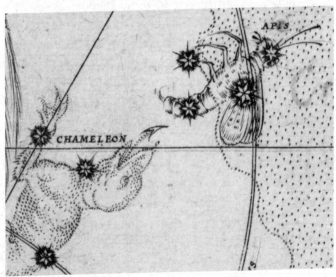

The constellation Apis, near the Southern Cross, in a detail from
an illustration in Johann Bayer, *Uranometria* (1603).

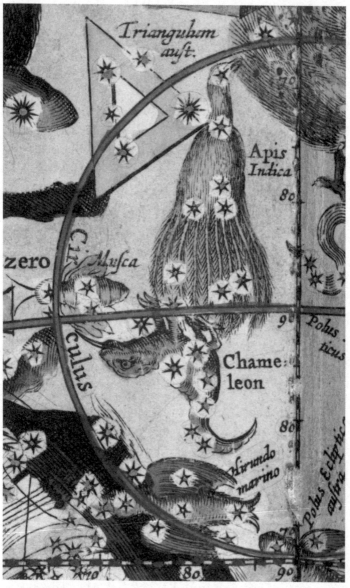

By the 1660s, Apis had become Musca ('fly') in Andreas Cellarius's
Harmonia Macrocosmica (1662).

Demeter were also styled melissae, and Ephesian Artemis was a many-breasted bee goddess, an iconograph almost certainly connected with the use of honey as a ritual or divine food, especially in baptism and other 'acceptance' rites among some Asian religions and in palaeo-Christian practice. For this reason, also, smearing oneself with honey wards off evil spirits.

The tradition of 'tanging' bees – calling them into a hive by beating on metal implements – may have arisen out of some of these stories. The Curetes, warrior-priests who with the melissae helped protect Zeus from Kronos, disguised the infant's cries by beating on their shields. Dionysus, who taught the art of bee-keeping to men, was originally a god of mead, not wine, and the cymbals and clashing revels of his cult were said to attract bees. Bacchus, like Dionysus also at first a god of mead rather than wine, according to Ovid, was the discoverer of honey. He was on his way to Rhodope when his attendants clashed their cymbals and some bees turned up, attracted by the noise. Bacchus shut them in a hollow tree where they made honey; and in a related story, Silenus, father of the satyrs, tried to rob a honey tree but was stung for his pains. Bacchus showed him how to relieve the hurt by rubbing honey on his wounds.[3] The belief in tanging bees is surprisingly persistent: in 1820 the misadventures of the inept Dr Syntax included an unfortunate encounter with tanged bees who insist on trying to settle in Syntax's wig rather than in the hive.[4]

By tradition, kept bees were never treated like other livestock but were more like members of the family, and important civilities and rituals involving them had to be observed. They must be told of the death of the bee keeper immediately, lest they abandon their hive for a new home. Whittier's 'Telling the Bees' has a bereaved lover remembering the day when, walking toward the house of his young lady, he saw the servant-girl laying scraps of black cloth on

Dr Syntax's wig is mistaken for a hive by bees being tanged by household servants (William Combe, *Doctor Syntax's Three Tours*, illustrated by Thomas Rowlandson (1868)).

each beehive. 'I knew she was telling the bees of one/ Gone on the journey we all must go!', he recalls, and the song the girl sang has lingered in his mind since – '"Stay at home, pretty bees, fly not hence!/ Mistress Mary is dead and gone!"'[5] More pleasant occasions such as marriage were also shared by the bees, who were offered food from the wedding feast.

The fastidiousness of bees (who hate bad breath, the odour of yew trees and any hint of onions) is probably the distant origin of one of the most amusing and improbable bee legends. It concerns the African ratal or honey badger (*Mellivora capensis*), which loves to eat honey, beeswax and bee larvae. The ratal will 'smoke' the bees out of their hive by farting into it. This resourceful animal, one of the few capable of digesting beeswax, is also said to steal beeswax candles from churches. Bees abhor bad language, and will sting those who swear in their presence; and they will drink only pure water.[6] This purity in the theological symbolics of bees extends such

The Barberini trigon on the fountain in Piazza Barberini, Rome.

ideas. They are associated, as we have already seen, with the virginity of Mary, and in their humming and their flight patterns with the ascent of the soul to heaven; in Breton myth, bees are supposed to have been created from Christ's tears on the cross (a belief only credible to those unacquainted with Aristotle and Virgil); they are the tears of the god Ra in Egyptian myth.[7] They were said in the north of England to sing at midnight on Christmas morning. In England the Julian calendar was abandoned for the Gregorian in 1752, and doubtful bee keepers in Yorkshire noted that the bees persisted in singing on what would have been the old Christmas Eve, not the new one.[8] The love bees bore for the industrious human-ist scholar Ludovico Vives prompted them to build their hive under the leads outside his study in Corpus Christi College, Oxford, in the 1520s. The bees remained there for more than a century; Corpus's soubriquet is 'The College of Bees', and the presidents of the college have traditionally kept bees since then.[9]

Bees have a traditional association with prophecy and sooth-saying. The original temple at Delphi was said to have been built of beeswax and tended by bees (probably connected with the *Melissae* who were the protectors of Zeus and later the priestesses of several cults). On the day the great English antiquary William Dugdale was born a swarm of bees entered his father's garden, 'esteemed by some a happy presage on the behalf of the Babe'. The bees, the scientist William Lilly later told Dugdale, 'did foretell that the Infant should in time prove a prodigy of industry' and, indeed, the bees were quite correct about Dugdale.[10] Similarly prophetic was a swarm of bees which flew into the Vatican as the conclave of cardinals were choosing a new pope in 1623. The swarm alighted in the chamber where Maffeo Barberini was awaiting the outcome of the election. Since the Barberini family crest consisted of the trigon of bees, it was inevitable that Maffeo should have been duly appointed as Urban VIII. The Barberini trigon was subsequently incorporated into architecture and monuments throughout Rome. The settling of a swarm of bees in the pediment of the Capitol in Rome during the minority of Nero was an omen of catastrophe which prompted the Emperor's mother Agrippina to take control of her son, according to Tacitus;[11] Livy reports another portentous swarm in 208 BC in the forum at Casinum.[12] That prophetic, ominous talent of bees is the subject of one of Emily Dickinson's more solemn bee poems:

> The murmuring of bees has ceased;
> But murmuring of some
> Posterior, prophetic,
> Has simultaneous come –
> The lower metre of the year,
> When nature's laugh is done, –
> The Revelations of the book
> Whose Genesis is June.[13]

Here, bees are natural oracles of the seasons, weather prophets whom Dickinson links with the visionaries of the Bible.

The Mormons who migrated from Illinois to Utah in 1847 under the guidance of Brigham Young settled in the Great Salt Lake Valley, which they called 'deseret', from an Egyptian bee symbol of the land of Egypt itself, sometimes transliterated as 'dsrt' or 'deshret'. *The Book of Mormon* describes the wilderness travails of the Jaredites, the supposed ancient North American antecedents of the Mormons, as they sought a promised land, a journey on which 'they did also carry with them deseret, which . . . is honeybee, and thus they did carry with them swarms of bees'.[14] Ethnic and religious migrations, in the Bible and in the *Book of Mormon*, are associated with the swarming of bees, and the beehive became the emblem of Mormon political and social organization, with its traditions of communalism and plural marriage closely resembling certain received ideas about apian behaviour (even though polygamy is impossible in bees, because a drone dies after a single mating). Brigham Young's house in Salt Lake City is known as the Beehive House, and the state seal of Utah (which the Mormons initially campaigned to be named 'Deseret') has a beehive at its centre, with the motto 'Industry'; the state slogan is 'the beehive state'. A curious photograph exists of a group of Mormon bishops all dressed in bee-striped prisoners' uniforms on the occasion of

The state seal of Utah, and a Highway Patrol licence plate featuring a skep.

George Q. Cannon and the Mormon bishops at the
Utah Territorial Penitentiary.

their visit to the state penitentiary in 1888 to express solidarity with
one George Cannon, an imprisoned Mormon protester against
anti-polygamy laws. It may well be that they deliberately donned
these clothes also to suggest their affinity with the bee.

Certain folk beliefs about bees are strictly speaking true. Aristotle thought that bees were deaf, and it is now established that they
have no auditory equipment at all. Bees were said to be terrified
by thunder and lightning and, indeed, their sensitivity to electrical
fields is well known, even if we have no way of knowing whether
they experience fear. Folklore says they are vulnerable to snow-
blindness and often land on the snow when they are lost and so
die of cold;[15] and bees do have limited colour vision within a very
specific range: they mainly respond to white, yellow, blue and
black. A snow-covered landscape – if a bee were so unlucky as to
venture out in such weather – would obliterate their visual navigational landmarks. The evidence of dead bees in the snow is, however,

far likelier to be the unhappy result of winter cleansing flights in weather which is too cold. Worker bees will not defecate in the hive, but will quickly perish outside the hive at temperatures below 7°C, or 45°F, so cleansing flights are always potentially risky. If they do not cleanse, on the other hand, they die of nosema, a disease of the digestive system.

The aphrodisiac and consciousness-altering properties of honey were among the standard beliefs of the Hindus and the Moors. The *Rig Veda* tells how Vishnu created a mead-spring from one of his footprints, and the mead made those who drank it highly fertile. It is more probable that the alcoholic content of mead, not the honey itself, was responsible for the weakening of sexual inhibitions, which resulted in pregnancy. Finnish myths in the Kalevala feature the bee as a heroic small bird who fetches honey to make beer ferment and to annoint the ill.[16]

There are plenty of purely fanciful ideas about bees that have no tangential relation to the truth. According to Virgil, they ballast

Peasants drunk on mead, from Olaus Magnus, *Historia de gentibus septentrionalibus* (1555).

A cunning bear drowns the bees to get at the honey (Diego di Saavedra Fajardo, *Idea Principis* (1640)).

CONSILIA MEDIA FVGIENDA

themselves for flight with tiny stones carried in their feet, a claim still being made in the 1680s by a leading member of the Royal Society.[17] If caught outdoors at nightfall and forced to camp out, Pliny explained, bees sleep on their backs in order to protect their wings from the dew.[18] For the Celts and the Saxons, bees were winged messengers between worlds, and the Egyptians represented *ka* (the soul) in the form of a bee. Crocodiles love honey and can only be fended off with saffron placed in front of the hive.[19] The Thonga people of Africa, as well as the Greeks, forbade the eating of honey by women until a year after marriage to prevent them from taking off like foraging bees. In Lithuania, it was claimed, there were large cavities in the earth which the 'infinite company of bees' in the region filled with honey, and bears apparently sometimes fell in and drowned.[20] On the other hand, cunning bears were also said to steal skeps and drown the bees in order to get the honey.

Men wishing to grow their beards quickly were advised by the sixteenth-century naturalist Ulisse Aldrovandi to rub their chins with the ashes of burnt bees, and the scientist Nehemiah Grew, a century later, was promoting bee-ash in preparations for hair-growth.[21] The Latin word for 'deceit' is also the word for 'drone', and the stingless drones, *fuci* or sham bees, were said to be those born late in the season and imperfect because the workers were too exhausted by this time to make complete bees. Bees who have died of the plague can be resuscitated by covering them with ashes of fig and warming them slightly.[22] If this operation is unsuccessful, the mixture of bees and fig-ash can be used as a medicine against pain and 'stoppages' (the anti-costive agent is of course the figs, not the bees).[23]

Our own bee traditions are strongly inflected by our history of keeping bees, but the techniques of bee- and honey-hunting have produced ancillary folk traditions. The European honeybee, known to the North American tribes as 'the Englishman's fly',[24] is not indigenous to the New World, but after their introduction into Virginia in 1621 they spread across the continent very rapidly, and by the early nineteenth century they were well established in the middle west. An extensive description of professional honey-hunting in the wild in this period appears in James Fenimore Cooper's *The Oak Openings or The Bee-Hunter* (1848). In this novel the intrepid hero, nicknamed 'Ben Buzz' and 'Le Bourdon' ('the drone'), lives in a shanty known as Castle Meal (from 'Chateau au Miel'), and has a trusty mastiff called Hive. In a climactic episode in his dealings with hostile Chippewa and Ojibway he uses his method of bee-spotting – triangulating from the beelines of various foraging bees to discover their hollow trees – to persuade a group of threatening braves of his necromantic ability to talk to bees, who 'tell' him of the location of honey and incidentally of

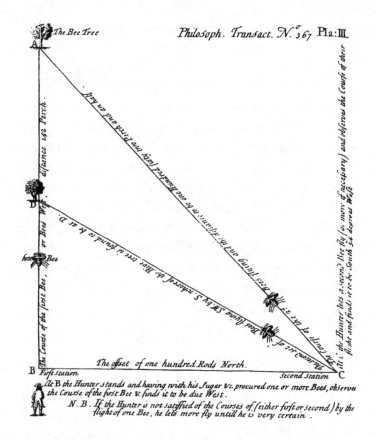

A diagram of triangulating for honey using beelines (Paul Dudley,
'An Account of a Method Lately Found Out in New-England for Discovering
Where the Bees Hive . . .', *Philosophical Transactions*, XXXI (1723)).

bears. The indians, who relish honey but do not understand the
principles of navigational geometry by which Le Bourdon discov-
ers bees, decide that he is a medicine man of great power. He uses
this influence to introduce them to Christianity and to the 'civil'
behaviour of the Europeans. Le Bourdon often moralizes on the life
of bees: the study of bees, like the study of wild things in general,
produces a Thoreauvian civility between white men and indians

which is natural and curiously American (the bad indians are, conveniently, those in the pay of the wily British in the upper Great Lakes). Like Sherlock Holmes, Le Bourdon establishes bee-hives of his own once he has retired from the frontier and established himself in a town with his wife and children. Gustave Aimard's *The Bee-Hunters* (1864) is set in Spanish California and features a Cooperesque misanthropic frontiersman who regards 'my fellow creatures [as] the wild-beasts of the prairie. What have I in common with you men of towns and cities, natural enemies of every being that breathes the pure air of liberty?'[25]

The bee of folklore has over the centuries garnered superstitions closely related to its political or Virgilian reputation for civility, its piety and blessedness, and the ongoing mystery of its natural history. There is another bee, however, of post-Enlightenment origin, a bee with a more relaxed attitude toward work, a bee which even, on occasion, displays a sense of humour.

nine

Playful Bee

Bees, as we know, both dance and sing, after a fashion, and the singing and dancing anthropomorphized bees in popular culture are exceptionally cute. Insects and other animals most remote from human form are most therionic – wild, alien – and often lack the apparently sentient facial expressions and behaviours of mammals. They are less likely to be projected as friendly, cuddly and emotionally intelligible. Admirable it may be, and a paragon among social insects, but the ant's shiny, brittle carapace is not cuddly; and most cartoon insects, with the joyful exception of Disney's Jiminy Cricket, are funny or villainous, but not adorable: one insect epic, *Antz*, starred the voice of Woody Allen in a predictably neurotic and stringy formic hero, with Gene Hackman as General Mandible.

The cuteness of cartoon animals and babies, according to Richard Klein, is produced by three coexistent qualities: they are small, plump, and cunningly contrived.[1] Cartoon characters with big eyes and long eyelashes, like Disney's Bambi, are sympathetic, especially if they are furry too. As in many other areas, the bee crosses over from theriomorph to anthromorph. Fuzzy and round with big eyes, the honeybee's and especially the bumble-bee's exopthalmic, neotenic, furry body signals it as friendly, soft and harmless. The Victorians, great cultivators of the excessively senti-mental, prospered a vogue for cute bee vignettes, such as Henry

A. Beers' tale of a drunken bumblebee who has had a few honey toddies too many:

> The golden sash about his body
> Scarce kept in his swollen belly
> Distent with honeysuckle jelly.
> Rose liquor and the sweet-pea wine
> Had fill'd his soul with song divine.[2]

But even for the careless bumblebee, the morning after the night before has to be reckoned with, and his tipsy song becomes a 'grumbling in low soft bass – poor maudlin bumble!' Walt Whitman, the unlikely admirer of this poem, describes in an essay of his own a heavy summer's day when he was

> envelop'd in the deep musical drone of these bees, flitting, balancing, darting to and fro about me by hundreds – big fellows with light yellow jackets, great glistening swelling

The cuteness of real bees.

The cartoon bee: small, plump, and cunningly contrived.

bodies, stumpy heads and gauzy wings . . . how it all nourishes, lulls me . . . up and down the lane, the darting, droning, musical bumble-bees. A great swarm again for my entourage as I return home, moving along with me as before . . . [S]eeking the sweet juice in the blossoms, [the tulip tree] swarms with myriads of these wild bees, whose loud and steady humming makes an undertone to the whole . . . [3]

Emily Dickinson liked grave, portentous bees, on the whole, but she was not immune to the charm of the 'buccaneer of buzz', and with this soubriquet noted the agreeable purring voice of the bee, its other almost mammalian attribute. In one of her best-known poems she alternates somewhat sentimental vignettes of flower-visits with the almost heroic capability of her poet/bee in a declaration of intellectual freedom from the lingering constraints of American Puritanism:

I taste a liquor never brewed,
From Tankards scooped in Pearl;
Not all the Vats upon the Rhine
Yield such an Alcohol!

Inebriate of Air am I,
And Debauchee of Dew,
Reeling, through endless summer days,
From inns of Molten Blue.

When 'Landlords' turn the drunken Bee
Out of the Foxglove's door,
When Butterflies renounce their drams,
I shall but drink the more!

Till Seraphs swing their snowy Hats,
And Saints to windows run,
To see the little Tippler
Leaning against the Sun![4]

She imagines herself as a bee who has slipped the stern work-ethic of her species; and the hive, with its longstanding connection with the humourless Calvinism of her forebears in New England, is latent in the image of an intoxicated and lounging bee. Dickinson, who also imagined a nectar-quaffing and pollen-pilfering bee 'exhilarated' by 'oriental heresies', would perhaps have approved the development by late-twentieth-century American microbreweries of 'honey beer' – not mead, and certainly not the tipple of bees, but a kind of adulterated beer for the modern, sweet-loving palate – and might even have rejoiced in the introduction by Young's, the London brewer, of a designer honey beer called 'Waggledance' ('One sip and

The drunken bee, from Robert Frankum, *The Bee and the Wasp: A Fable* (1832).

George Cruikshank fec.

your taste buds will be dancing all day') – one of the few instances in which a product-branding exercise seems to have incorporated a genuine feature of apian honeymaking. Honey was the downfall of a country bumblebee beguiled by a wily urban wasp in a poem of 1832 by Robert Frankum which borrows the antique theme of the country mouse and the city mouse. The portly bee finally dies of an apoplexy brought on by overindulgence in his own brew.[5]

In Arthur Askey's wacky 'Bee Song' bees are ridiculed for collecting pollen from cauliflowers and building honeycombs that look like tripe. But however cock-eyed imagined bee-labour becomes, they always remain civil: 'Bees in a beehive must behive', Askey proclaims.[6] W. S. Gilbert created a comic 'one is not amused' style of Victorian queen bee. Her workers suggest 'with due submission' that a nice bit of swarming might be in order, but her response is disappointing:

The queen bee, from Waldemar Bonsels, *Maya the Bee* (1920).

Up spake their Queen and thus spake she –
'This is a matter that rests with me,
Who dares opinions thus to form?
I'll tell you when it is time to swarm!'
Buzz, buzz, buzz, buzz.

Her Majesty wore an angry frown,
In fact Her Majesty's foot was down –
Her Majesty sulked – declined to sup –
In short, Her Majesty's back was up.
Buzz, buzz, buzz, buzz.[7]

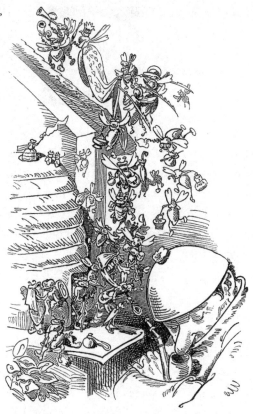

The queen's flight, from Wilhelm Busch, *Buzz a Buzz, or the Bees.*

An obstinate bee named Peter reminds his comrades that they are not to bow to tyranny, and proposes to swarm by himself if no one will join him. The queen and the other bees decide that the solitary swarming Peter has been at the sherry again, the only explanation for his antic behaviour. Generally, bees do behave, but they can also be annoying, as for Edward Lear's old man of Tralee 'who was horribly bored by a bee'. This regular brute of a bee's only crime was to buzz, leaving us quite out of sympathy with the truculent Irishman; for poets, and most of us, the humming of bees is the delightful sound-track of summer and verdancy.[8]

The upright Do-Bee from the American TV series *Romper Room*.

Until the twentieth century there were few really brutish bees in the popular imagination, and Edward Lear is clearly playing with the bee's longstanding reputation for virtue. The bee's anthropomorphized valiance is genuinely transformed, however, into satirical edge in Robert Kirk's 1937 epigram about a rival who could not be injured by the poet's lampoon against him but felt keenly the pain of a bee's sting:

> Poets are witty men like me,
> But only God can make a bee![9]

This bee, whose sting is more effective than any lampoon, is still a righteous bee who punctures the poet's enemy, but also the pretensions of the poet himself. The bee as a pointed satirist was converted for the children of cold-war America into a more gently didactic force in the upright Do-Bee, a character in the long-running American children's television programme of the 1960s and '70s, *Romper Room*. The Do-Bee (an animated bee and also an actor in a bee-suit) exhorted children to behave with courtesy and thoughtfulness. Good children were Do-Bees and naughty ones were Don't-Bees (played by frowning, grouchy bees). 'Do Be a Do-Bee and Don't Be a Don't-Bee' went the mantra, and little children (including the author) paid attention. *Romper Room* is no more, but in consolation today's young children can have a 'Bee Attitude' rug at home or at school, a rug full of smiling bees urging them to 'bee polite', 'bee cheerful' and 'bee kind', or they can attend one of the Bee Attitude Schools, run by an American Christian educational foundation. The punsters of 'bee-attitude' tend, unfortunately, to confuse the Commandments with the Beatitudes. The comedian Jerry Seinfeld, one of the late baby-boom generation which grew up with *Romper Room*, plays the lead in *Bee Movie*, set in an anthropomorphic bee world which resembles Manhattan. The ancient tradition flourishes even here: in a press release Seinfeld explained that he is 'fascinated by bee society, the world's most harmoniously run organization, and now I finally am going to be in it'.[10]

ten

Bee Movie

We call them the killer bees
The Sandinistas call them their 'freedom fighters'
An evil empire of godless Marxist bugs
How can they be stopped? . . .
And as they spread their Marxist pollen from flower to flower,
They corrupt our pure, all-American bees . . .
Remember, America, these are red bees, all workers,
no drones!
The Bobs, 'Killer Bees' (1988)[1]

At what point does the bee begin to acquire the baggage of threat, distaste and horror? Insects, especially after the microscopic revolution of the 1660s, began to appear as figures of revulsion in Augustan writing, their now-magnified anatomies on display in the careful engravings of the naturalists. Robert Hooke's *Micrographia* (1665) shows a magnified flea and louse, the flea's picture more than a foot long and a foot high, the louse a spectacular two feet long. Pope, Swift, Gibbon and Burke express their disgust at the 'immoral or dirty Actions' of swarms, hordes and contemptibly 'industrious Bugs':[2] in *Letter to a Noble Lord* (1795) on the French Revolution, Burke converts the ancient miracle of the ox-born bee into insurrectionary insects who emerge irresistibly 'from the rotten carcass of their own murdered country'.[3] Insects had always been vermin; now, however, they acquired a terrifying ugliness. Milton's swarms of damned angels, commanded by Beelzebub, literally 'the lord of flies', haunted the body and the imagination.

Bees and ants had, however, usually been excluded from this opprobrium, and so the comprehensive metamorphosis of the exemplary, dutiful bee of the pre-modern era into the terrifying swarm of the twentieth-century horror flick is clearly of a different pattern altogether. It starts, obliquely, with the Romantic critique of the industrial revolution: Coleridge, Carlyle, Wordsworth and Ruskin, the so-called 'Romantic ecologists',[4] made an oppositional reading of nature/manufacture, agriculture/industry, outdoor/ indoor, to illustrate the effect of industrialization on individual freedom and happiness. In *The Excursion* Wordsworth disparages the factory where each individual puts on the yoke of a repetitive, brutalizing, bestial task, denied 'what there is delightful in the breeze, / The gentle visitations of the sun'.[5] Ruskin abhors the division of labour which divides humans into 'mere segments of men – broken into small fragments and crumbs of life', which isolates them from any communal or social impulse or result.[6]

This expression of anxiety at the power and human cost of the industrial process and the capitalist impulse that impels it, which convert the individual into an interchangeable part in a huge production machine, often alludes to the features of apian social organization that were increasingly troubling nineteenth-century observers. The bee, once the uncontested emblem of moral rectitude in its communal cooperation, was now starting to be understood as radically, unnervingly 'unselfed', a natural emblem of the anonymous and identical part in a hive which quickly began to resemble nothing so much as a mill or a foundry. The development of modern apiculture, dating from Langstroth's 1851 invention of the movable-frame hive and other innovations, seemed,

In this cartoon, attributed to William Dent, the right-hand figure is said to be Edmund Burke, an eloquent opponent of the French Revolution, overturning a beehive, a symbol of the French Republic (1786).

moreover, to industrialize beekeeping itself, so that the mid- and late-nineteenth-century hive really did suggest a factory, where, as Blake said, 'the Arts of Life they chang'd into the Arts of Death'.[7] Carlyle compared the working of the metal in a sheet-iron mill to the manipulation of beeswax.[8]

Coleridge, writing of mob behaviour, said that crowds, 'like bees . . . become restless and irritable through the increased temperature of collected multitudes. Hence the German word for fanaticism is derived from the swarming of bees, namely, *Schwaermen, Schwaermerey*.'[9] At least from the 1780s, the disobedient mob and its actions, the unruly crowd governed by political or social grievance, was particularly horrifying. Carlyle and Burke also used *schwärmerei* ('to swarm', or, metaphorically, to show extravagant enthusiasm, to rave) to describe the mob-led events of the French Revolution. The sense of deathly, impersonal, and uncontrollable industrial processes combines with this fear of the crowd and its 'selfless' mechanisms, to be sustained and extended in the later, mechanized, electronic vision of modern social organization where 'consciousness and self-control are lost [to] the occult, the superstate, the megamachine for living . . ., the logic of technique . . . [T]he culture becomes a machine, and whenever a human being willingly merges with, or joins his being to that of a machine, that's the formula for death.'[10]

Edward Paley's anti-Luddite tract of 1831 encouraged workers to accept new industrial processes with a fable about bees who misuse a wonderful honey-making machine and get into difficulties through riotous behaviour and bad management. They have only themselves and not their machine to blame, their queen tells them. The moral: 'machinery is the friend, not the antagonist of man. It works that he may *rest*, not that he may be *idle* . . . It enriches the wealthy for the benefit of the poor.'[11] The same industrial and economic logic of the modern era is eerily represented by David Wojahn's poem 'The Hivekeepers', which opens with a reference to Breughel's painting on that subject. Their bee suits, it transpires, remind the poet of the protective gear which is fatally absent from the Polish asbestos-removers in New York City, workers who rejoice in their new American prosperity but who are already showing symptoms of the asbestosis or mesothelioma that will kill them. The asbestos removed from apartment walls on the West Side is compared to 'ungainly slabs of honey', and that grim mortality of honey and of bees here becomes the pitiless and noxious history of a dangerous industrial product and of the practices which sacrificed workers to corporate profit.[12]

The unsettling truth about bees did not, however, establish a monolithic attitude of distaste. A. I. Root, a professional American beekeeper, was not happy that bees were associated with violence and rage. In his encyclopaedia entry 'Anger of Bees' (where he oddly characterizes them as male), he writes:

> Bees are, on the contrary, the pleasantest, most sociable, genial and good-natured little fellows one meets in all animated creation . . . Why, we can tear their beautiful comb all to bits right before their very eyes; and without a particle of resentment, but with all the patience in the world they will at once set to work to repair it, and that, too, without a word of remonstrance.[13]

Indeed, practical apiarists like Root and Langstroth were more or less immune to the developing aesthetic of the troubling, enslaved or mindless bee that informed the thought of the Romantics, and which would colour work on bees from the turn of the twentieth century. The Reverend Lorenzo Langstroth patented his movable-frame hive in the 1850s, but then published the design widely so that anyone could copy it – a signal and almost apian act of self-lessness and charity. Amos Root explicitly linked his beekeeping with his Christianity. His firm, which still operates from Medina, Ohio, pioneered the package-bee industry, the production of high-quality beekeeping equipment, candles, and a publishing house which began to produce *The ABC and XYZ of Bee Culture* in 1884, and updates it to this day; Root Industries is still known as an almost godly enterprise in the style of the seventeenth-century Puritans. Hart Crane, however, combined the newer, disturbing recognition of the relentless and merciless machinery of the hive with the older, theological associations of bees: the human heart is 'the hive of the world' which, for all its pain and anguish, issues in mercy, honey and golden love.[14] In the past two centuries, in short,

The Hivekeepers (1560s) by Pieter Breughel the Elder.
This ink drawing is also said to be of honey-thieves.

the emblematics of the bee have become unstable, with poets like Crane able to invoke simultaneously the good Virgilian bee and an emerging bad or troublingly impersonal bee.

After several millennia of bee legend, in which the insect has been credited with an enormous range of the admirable qualities we most respect in human beings, we are well used to the charming fantasies which explained the extraordinary social organization of the bee by means of human behaviour, philosophy and faith. The bee's special qualities were perceived as emblems of spatial, social and moral order. Until the mid-nineteenth century, the countlessness of bees had not yet been converted into the threatening crowd, the mob whose collective will is both unassailable and unaccountable. What Coleridge had defined in 1817 as 'passion . . . in inverse proportion to insight' was in the twentieth century extended by Elias Canetti in his influential theory of the crowd. Bee society is eerily, inadvertently, described by such a theory: the colony always wants to grow, although, unlike the crowd, it can be contained and managed consensually by keeper and bees. The equality of all members of a crowd evolves rapidly in the dangerous selflessness of the mob. This equality is expressed in the hive, where, except for the remote and cloistered queen, bees have no perceptible hierarchy. The density of crowds and of bees is similar and, as Canetti says, a crowd is (or feels) densest at the moment of discharge into action. A swarm of bees is a purposeful discharge into action, its common goal (to find a new nest-site) activating each member; when the swarm reaches its goal it changes its behaviour. The crowd, like the swarm, exists only so long as its goal is unattained, and Canetti proposes that the fear of disintegration will allow the crowd to accept *any* goal. It is because bees are subject to crowd mentality and behaviour – which are their own end and purpose – that they successfully reproduce by division when they swarm.[15]

As long ago as the eighteenth century, when microscopy was advanced enough and naturalists disinterested enough to detect the true facts about bees, it was increasingly clear that bee-fables were to be relegated to the category of allegory, children's stories and crude folk belief. The important experimental work of Sir John Lubbock, 1st Baron Avebury, in the 1870s on the social insects seems after so long a history of political bee-lore sadly but necessarily neutral. Because Lubbock and others suspected that bees must possess powers of communication, he tried to find out, by measuring its intelligence, how a bee can tell its comrades the location of food without actually leading them to it (the answer lies, of course, in the dances described by von Frisch). Lubbock's experiments were inconclusive, and he gave up because not one of his trial bees seemed able or inclined to bring its friends to the waiting food. Nor was Lubbock interested in the potential emotional organization of bees, other than to dismiss them as too excitable to work with experimentally and to note that thundery weather puts them 'much out of humour'.[16] He does, however, quote the venerable Revd Langstroth, inventor of the modern hive, on the bee's complete lack of conscience in robbing other bees:

There is an air of roguery about a thieving bee which, to the expert, is as characteristic as are the motions of a pickpocket to a skilful policeman. Its sneaking look and nervous, guilty agitation, once seen, can never be mistaken.[17]

Neither Lubbock nor Langstroth explains how a bee can look guilty. Lubbock also quotes Langstroth on the bee's eagerness for honey:

No one can understand the extent of their infatuation until he has seen a confectioner's shop assailed by myriads of hungry bees. I have seen thousands strained out from the syrup in which they perished; thousands more alighting even upon the boiling sweets; the floor covered and windows darkened with bees, some crawling, others flying, and others still so completely besmeared as to be able neither to crawl or fly – not one in ten able to carry home its ill-gotten spoils, and yet the air filled with new hosts of thoughtless others.[18]

It may be no more than coincidence, but Lubbock's other significant contribution was the invention of the bank holiday in 1871, in a Parliamentary act designed to ensure the rights of shopworkers, in whose welfare he interested himself greatly. That bees observe no holidays and carry out their work unremittingly may have inspired Lubbock's political convictions.

The queen bee is marked by her size and by the red dot painted on her thorax.

With this normally neutral experimental and practical work on bees by Langstroth and Lubbock as well as Johann Dzierzon, Charles Dadant, A. I. Root, Moses Quinby, François Huber and others in the public domain for some years, it is surprising to read Maurice Maeterlinck's turn-of-the-twentieth-century rhapsody about the wonderful polity of the hive and relentless anthropomorphizing the insect itself. His immensely popular *The Life of the Bee* (1901) mingles a rather naïve romanticism with some of the latest information from the scientists, and this curious amalgam wavers – reluctantly, it seems – between his own practical understanding of bees and the irresistible poetic urge to characterize bees as equipped with human intelligence and emotion. The lesson of the bees, he informs us, is that of 'ardent and disinterested work' – the same lesson we have learned from Hesiod onward. It is born out of a mystical sense of what he calls 'the genius of the hive': this is the 'vaster although less perceptible principle' of futurity.[19] 'The god of the bees is the future', Maeterlinck declares; it is for the successful preservation of and extension of the generations and thus of the hive itself as a corporate entity that the individual bee subsumes itself in the anonymous business of the multitude, that it works itself to death for honey it will never taste and children it will never bear.[20] He rightly observes that the more organized a society the more circumscribed become individual freedoms, an important Hobbesian truth very efficiently demonstrated by the beehive, where the 'virgin daughters of toil', as he calls them, forego 'love' and procreation in exchange for domestic, economic and political security. His fascinating – and occasionally crackpot – analysis of apian behaviour leads him to extremes of admiration and melancholy, and the book is designed to alert us to 'the almost perfect but pitiless society of our hives, where the individual is entirely merged in the republic, and the republic in its turn invariably sacrificed to the abstract and immortal city of the future'.[21] The hive, he proclaims, behaves according to laws superior to its own happiness, and he is supremely impressed with what he calls the 'heroic renouncement' which is made by swarming bees in abandoning their safe and well-established hive for new, initially barren lodgings.[22] This 'moral tradition of the hive' prompts him to what might be described as a transitional attitude to bees, an attitude arising from the conventional (and comfortable) tradition of the civil bee, the bearer of altruistic and sisterly messages of disinterested good will and common well-being, and at the same time from an emerging (and uncomfortable) vision of social insects – and the bee in particular – as a threatening, machine-like, heedless, thoughtless member of an irrational crowd.[23]

A slightly later instalment of this transitional attitude is offered by Rudolf Steiner's bee symbolics: in making honey, he claims, bees distill and concentrate cosmic forces which are imbibed by those who ingest honey, and he links the gestational periods of the different castes of bee (quite meaninglessly) by numerology to elemental forces. Thus the worker's 21-day gestation, equivalent to the sun's period of rotation on its axis, makes her a 'sun animal', the drone is an 'earth animal', and the queen, whose gestation at 16 days is less than the sun's 21, must be a 'sun child'. Although this Steinerian bee has something in common with the much older belief that bees are divine messengers, still the insect has been de-personalized, not as a machine but as an instrument and bearer of power from vital but impersonal elemental forces. What exactly Steiner thought he was offering to the Swiss beekeepers in his audience (beekeepers of Dornach, not far, as it happens, from La Chaux-de-Fonds), and what they made of it, is not recorded.[24] It is, however, an interesting modern example of the way bees have throughout the history of thought been loaded with moral and abstract meanings.

Both Maeterlinck and Steiner provide us with interesting historical perspectives. Maeterlinck's simultaneous enthusiasm for and dismay about the nature of bees takes its cue not only from the Romantics, but also from the sort of Utopian schemes, including Marx's, which yielded the exhilaration of 1917 and eventually the horror of Stalinist communism. Steiner, fomenting a quasi-philosophical cult two decades later, seems to jettison actual knowledge of the real life of bees (which he demonstrably possessed) to make room for entirely arbitrary assertions apparently designed to fascinate his clientele without actually offering them anything of practical use. The decline of utility in discussions of the bee is the signal development in twentieth-century apian discourse.

A Bad Bee fully emerges in the second half of the twentieth century, associated with two historical events. The first was biological. It was long established that the western honey-bee did not thrive particularly well in sub-tropical and tropical regions

Donald Gill's bees had been destroyed by bad weather in Cache County, Utah, in the late 1930s. A rehabilitation loan from the Farm Security Administration helped him to re-start his business.

and, because of this, the Brazilian geneticist Warwick Kerr was trying in the mid-1950s to find a way to improve honey-production in South America. He had heard of very high rates of production achieved by South African beekeepers in similar climatic conditions, using the African subspecies *Apis mellifera scutellata*. These bees were known to be more aggressive than their western counterparts, but he calculated that by interbreeding the two, the hybrid bee would be gentler than the African parent while retaining its high production capacity in the torrid zone. In 1956, Kerr imported queens from South Africa and Tanzania, 35 of which were ultimately selected for breeding in Brazil. In 1957, the new hybrid colonies headed by the African queens were placed in the Saõ Paolo forest and began to reproduce, the new bees all 'Africanized' hybrids. By one of those blandly ordinary but catastrophic accidents, one of the caretakers removed the entrance guards (the simple piece of hardware that confines the large queen to the hive), and 26 of the Africanized colonies swarmed.

These swarms of Afro-western bees did not behave as predicted: many of the most important traits of the European parent were recessive, and instead they displayed the extraordinary behaviour inherited from the African parent that marks out their brilliant adaptive capabilities. The purpose of modern hive-structure, with its added supers on top of the main hive, serves to keep colonies of bees at home because it offers a successful colony ever more space to rear brood and store honey. A swarm of bees is a large contingent of a colony which has grown too big for its existing nest, and this contingent leaves the nest with the established queen to find a new site in which to locate another colony, leaving the old, now-diminished, nest to hatch a new queen and replenish the number of workers. Thus, swarming is a form of reproduction by division, and is heavily discouraged by beekeepers, who of course prefer to have their bees stay at home and put their energies into honey production rather than into reproduction. The Africanized colonies were going to disappoint: as subsequent research has shown, tropical bee species are not only more aggressive, but are programmed to reproduce rapidly by colony division. With no winter to get through, tropical bees have no environmental pressure to lay up large stores of honey, so the opportunity provided by modern supers to extend storage space is meaningless to this new kind of bee. But with predation a key impulse in their genetic and adaptive make-up, Africanized bees *are* programmed to reproduce much more rapidly than their western cousins (and large honey stores not only attract predators, but need maintenance which compromises the colony's ability to rear enough brood to allow for division by swarming). The swarming mechanism is the means (or the consequence) of this high reproductivity, and it is the strong tendency to swarm which has expressed itself in the hybrid bee, and which has determined the steady expansion of its territory: since the initial escape in 1957, the western bee population in South America has gradually been hybridized in the wild as the new bees have spread, and that range has expanded at the rate of 300–500 km per year, to include French Guiana by 1975, southern Mexico by 1986 and southern Texas by 1990. In 2002 Africanized bees had colonized southern California, southern Nevada, Arizona and southern New Mexico. Some scientists expect them to move farther east and north of this, but their progress will eventually be halted by the climate – they do not store sufficient honey to survive the winter months – but where they have already spread they present certain problems which have been much magnified in the popular imagination. Although their venom is no more potent than the western bee's, their aggression exhibits itself in occasional mass attacks, and they will chase a perceived predator for as much as a kilometre. Neither of these behaviours is seen in the western bee. Although the incidence of mass attacks on humans is in fact very low (2.1 deaths per million by one estimate), the Africanized hybrids have acquired an almost mythic reputation as 'killer bees'.[25]

The second event in the conversion of bees into monsters was a political trend. In post-war America, hysterical fear of Communist incursion – military and psychological – was epidemic, the so-called 'American' values of individual liberty and conscience pitched against a caricatured model of socialism in which the individual was utterly subdued to the will of the state. At this time a Stalinist entomologist in the Soviet Union was busy excoriating an American entomologist for suggesting that the bee colony operates like a Wall Street corporation governed by a board of 'secret bees' who control public opinion; he congratulated his compatriot

Children tasting honey on a Soviet farming collective in
the Altai territory of Central Asia, *c.* 1930s.

beekeepers for recognizing that, at what he calls 'the end of the
capitalist epoch', nature observes no such bourgeois structures.
Bees, he argued, would in their radical, communist civility assist
the Soviet peoples in the ideological and the agricultural struggle
to refashion the earth.[26]

The implicit likeness of bees to the evil socialist hordes was
adapted by Hollywood in its typically explicit style. Beginning in
the 1950s, horror and science fiction films feature bees as monsters, either as the giant bees of *Mysterious Island* (1951; remade
in 1961), the tiny automata now big enough to make comb with
man-sized cells and powerful enough to capture and incarcerate
the intrepid heroes of the story. The mechanization of human
labour, fear of the mob, the rise of scientific socialism and latterly
the amalgam of anti-communist and racist sentiments, haunt the
history of film, and this potent combination of ideas coalesces
initially in popular, disturbing images of insects in general and
later of bees in particular. Fritz Lang's Wellsian *Metropolis* (1927)

The city of the future as a beehive in Fritz Lang's 1927 film *Metropolis*.

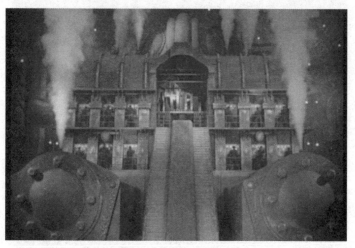

Workers in their cells in *Metropolis*.

imagines a future city of the year 2000 whose workers are enslaved in underground factories where they perform repetitive tasks enclosed in tiny, stacked cells. The rigorous order of the hive and the comb in obedience to an overarching national imperative was

Workers as bees in *Metropolis*.

later captured by Leni Riefenstahl in *Triumph of the Will* (1935) with pictures of Nazi rallies. Political and social metaphors, always so easily attached to the bee and to the hive, by this moment clearly become disquieting. Victor Erices's cult film *El Espiritu de la Colmena* (*The Spirit of the Beehive*) (1973), set in the early days of Franco's regime, adapts this disquiet specifically to bees, the frequent cutaway shots to a glass beehive and the voiceover of the anti-Fascist beekeeper recognizing that the gentle civility and industry of bees under a benevolent queen is doomed in the wasteland of tyranny; and the relentlessly communal behaviour of the bees is both exhilarating and troubling in its total absence of personal will or desire. The beehive becomes a figure for the entrapment of the workers under Franco, and an equivocal metaphor of the Republican spirit.

The mob killer and the communist swarm coalesced in horror films during the 1960s. *We Shall See* (1964), based on an Edgar

Wallace novel, has a murder by bee-stings, and *The Deadly Bees* (1967) (by Robert Bloch, writer of *Psycho*), pits a good beekeeper against an evil one who is raising a killer strain. In both, the bees are merely the instruments of malicious human agents, a theme continued in *Killer Bees* (1974), the first of two movies of that name. This outlandish story stars Gloria Swanson as a manipulative matriarch who has psychic control of the bees in her vineyard, and continues the metaphor of the queen bee as a malevolent and tyrannical force which had already featured in the 1955 Joan Crawford vehicle *Queen Bee*, whose character ruthlessly manipulates others in her orbit. *Invasion of the Bee Girls* (1972) stars a coven of women who use radiation-treated bee serum to take on apian characteristics, which in the film includes the post-coital killing of men. But the nasty queen bee lost ground in the horror-stakes to

The 1934 Nuremberg rally in Leni Riefenstahl's 1935 film
The Triumph of the Will.

Left: A publicity image for Alfredo Zacharias's 1978 film *The Bees*.
Right: A poster for *The Bees.*

the more irrational terror of the crowd in later bee films. The 1970s brought a rich and often kooky menu of bee horror, including *The Savage Bees* (1976), where killer bees decimate New Orleans during Mardi Gras, and the gloriously bad *The Swarm* (1978), in which Michael Caine watches bees kill soldiers, schoolchildren and picnicking families, attack a nuclear power plant and destroy Houston. Fortunately for Texas, the US Army Corps of Engineers figures out how to lure the bees to an oil slick in the Gulf of Mexico using foghorns that sound like the drone's mating-call, and engulf them in a firestorm. The latent political bias of the film is given away by the immortal disclaimer in the credit sequence: 'the African killer bee portrayed in this film bears absolutely no relationship to the industrious, hard-working American honeybee'.[27] *Terror Out of the Sky* (1979) has yet more schoolchildren attacked by bees. The plot of the hilariously awful *The Bees* (1978) is so silly that it defies belief: the US is invaded by eco-warrior bees who want to save the environment and redress the unjust exploitation of their species. They disrupt a major football game by attacking thousands; they storm the United Nations headquarters in New York to present their case; they are finally thwarted by a hero-scientist who finds a chemical that turns bees into homosexuals.

The real schemes of governments to contain the northward spread of the real bees are, unfortunately, hardly less fanciful or horrifying: a malathion-impregnated 80-km-wide barrier zone in central America was proposed by the United States, as was a radiation belt, and a line of enormous gas-fuelled flame jets along the Panama Canal. Meanwhile, the popular alarmist Leonard Nimoy (aka Mr Spock of *Star Trek*, and thus authoritative) presented a sensational killer-bee documentary on American television in 1976, fuelling tabloid panic.

The taste for sudden and completely unaccountable apian savagery has hardly abated. Dario Argento's *Phenomena* (English title *Creepers*) (1985) is about a girl who can communicate with insects, including bees. In avenging a murder she is, as the film's trailer proclaims, able to call on the assistance of 'a few million of her closest friends' who swarm violently. *Candyman* (1992) is based on a Clive Barker story, with an urban legend about the ghost of a freed slave who dared to court a white girl. In punishment he was coated with honey by an outraged mob, stung to death by bees, and has ever after haunted Cabrini Green in Chicago, one of the most deprived African-American urban ghettos in the country. The interesting conjunction here between unnerving mass behaviour (the bees, the murderous crowd) and fear of negritude ('africanized' bees, the setting in Cabrini Green) marries the underlying racial fear encoded in the killer-bee phenomenon with the somewhat older tradition of unruly rebellion. The slave's spirit lingers as 'the Candyman', accompanied (indeed, infested) by bees,

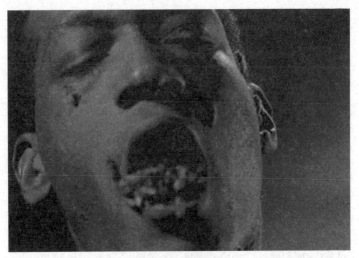

The corruptively produced bee in Bernard Rose's 1992 film *Candyman*.

to disembowel white women. The details are interesting and incendiary. In the legend, bees were the specific agents of the slave's death, suggesting the killer bee in action (even though bees, presented with a honey-coated object, will invariably assemble to retrieve the honey and take it back to the hive rather than sustain huge losses in the colony by pointlessly stinging); the victim is himself black, and like the vengeful killer bees his ghost is actuated by the will to vengeance against his oppressors. Barker's original story is set in Liverpool, and the idea came to him as he mused on the Tate & Lyle logo (bees emerging from the carcass of a lion). The striking publicity image of the Candyman has bees crawling out of his mouth, a carcass, apparently, bringing forth sweetness. The American film version, crude as it is in some ways, seems to be manipulating racial prejudice and racial guilt simultaneously, with fear of irrational violence on the one hand (especially by black men against white women) coupled with fear of racially motivated revenge, which is in some sense justifiable.

The African bee panic was satirized in the American television show *Saturday Night Live* by comedians in bee costumes behaving like surly, machine-gun-toting, Mexican bandito bees equipped with killingly bad jokes, by Michael Moore in *Bowling for Columbine* (2002), where the cartoon-within-the-film shows 'African' bees invading the United States, bringing with them the ghastly Communist ideology like a disease which breeds in the tropics, and by the *a capella* group The Bobs, whose song 'Killer Bees' is quoted at the head of this chapter. All these satires, interestingly, are produced by Americans of the northern tier (Michigan, New Hampshire, and various other north-eastern states) where there are no killer bees.

The godless Marxist bugs of an earlier American era were not entirely supplanted by the dark races – there remained, after all, bastions of political antagonism in Central and South America such as Castro in Cuba and Allende in Chile – but they were powerfully enhanced by the even more primal white American fear of its own African-American population. At about the same time, two further documentaries about the Africanized bees approaching the American border appeared – *Killer Bees* in 1992, and *The Swarm: India's Killer Bees* in 2000. In 1995, *Deadly Invasion: The Killer Bee Nightmare* followed killer bees chasing an innocent (white) Californian family, and *Killer Bees* (2002) – billed as '*Arachnophobia* with stingers' – shows swarthy Mexican pollinators bringing truck-loads of lethal bees into the Pacific northwest, where inevitably they wreak havoc on the community. The crisis, emerging from the accidental release of the wrong bees into the fruit groves, converts the usually beneficial behaviour of bees in servicing plants into a deadly symbiosis, and the arts of life become the arts of death. This crisis is not by any means imaginary: California, where the use of pollination services is huge, and the Gulf states, where commercial bee-breeding operations are based and from where package-bees are shipped, are all within the climatic limit of the Africanized bee, and its spread could have extremely serious consequences for American agriculture and food production. For this reason some parts of Texas where the bees have settled are now quarantined. The most recent bee movie shifts the familiar killer-bee role onto the wasp: in *Deadly Swarm* (2003) Africanized killer wasps escape from a medical experiment studying their venom, and of course cause mayhem. Most large-budget disaster movies have been set in the United States. In the case of the bee movie, there is unlikely to be a European contribution for the simple reason that the nearest aggressive Africanized bees are across the ocean.

With the break-up of the Soviet Union, moreover, the formerly charged image of the socialist or communist mob lost some of its power, but with entrenched latent American racism on hand to supply the void, the unholy glamour of Cold War them-or-us thrillers mutated into something utterly fantastic in the shape of *Wax: or the Discovery of Television Among Bees* (1992), quite possibly the strangest film ever made, and alarmingly listed by the Internet Movie Database as a documentary.[28] A computer programmer working at the weapons testing range at Alamogordo, New Mexico, is married to a woman significantly called Melissa, and is a beekeeper in his spare time. His bees (an invented 'Mesopotamian' strain) are in fact psychic bees who can import images into the mind of their keeper. Eventually they put a special bee 'television' in his head, causing him – not surprisingly – to hallucinate. The bees, who turn out to be the dead souls of the future, take him to their home underneath the desert where he is told he must become a weapon and hit a target in Iraq.

The benign, or at least the politically and emotionally meaningful, bee seems to be making a partial comeback. The African 'killer' bees reached the United States border in the 1990s with no appreciable threat to the American population, and the cosy re-assurance of the well-disposed apian polity has partly re-emerged in popular culture. The civil-bee metaphor began to surface again in 1982 with *La Colmena* (The Beehive), a gloomy story based on the novel by Cela, set in wartime Madrid. *O Melissokomos* (1986), starring Marcello Mastroianni as a retired schoolteacher trying to put some meaning into his life by becoming a beekeeper who eventually commits suicide by stinging, and *Ulee's Gold* (1997), starring Peter Fonda, revive the tradition thoroughly. Both are indebted to *The Keeper of the Bees* (1925), remade in 1935 and 1947, in which a disabled war veteran finds solace in beekeeping. *Ulee's Gold* is the somewhat melancholy story of a professional beekeeper whose criminal son and addict daughter-in-law have abandoned their children to him. Throughout the film, violent and unpleasant interludes with his dysfunctional family are punc-tuated by Ulee's careful rearing of his granddaughters and his necessary retreat into the quiet and strictly regulated world of bee-keeping. The processes of gathering and packing the honey become therapeutic for Ulee and his disordered family, and the gold of the title is not just the honey, but the reward of duty and moral intervention.[29]

Against these rather spare films, the literary bee is also back in fashion. Thomas McMahon's *McKay's Bees* (1979) follows the westward trek of an American inspired in 1855 by Langstroth's *On the Hive and Honey*. McKay wants to found a utopian bee-keeping community in Kansas (which will make clocks and music boxes in the winter). Under his aegis the transplanted bees rescue a Free-Soiler (an Abolitionist working to establish the new terri-tories in the west as non-slave states) by stinging his attacker to death – an interesting back-adaptation of the killer-bee theme for a much earlier period. 'Bees', McKay says, 'never let themselves fall into reveries of worry and speculation on their future. Instead, they conduct their affairs with confidence and optimism.'[30] In the Free-Soiler incident, the swarm seems instinctively to opt for the Abolitionist cause, perhaps in their own interest. More disturbing is the incestuous relationship between McKay's wife and her twin brother, specifically likened to the mating of a drone offspring with the queen. In contrast, in the folksy, feel-good morality of Sue Monk Kidd's bestselling *The Secret Life of Bees* (2002) (and the 2008 film), the fashionable themes of racial harmony, religious ecstasy and female empowerment and solidarity are gathered under the thematic umbrella of, again, therapeutic beekeeping. One of the central characters is an authoritative black woman who lives with her sisters and sells her gourmet honey under the 'Black Madonna' label deep in 1960s South Carolina; the religious iconography of bees in association with the Virgin Mary is never far from view. Against this, vegans have entered the debate about the efficiency of bees as pollinators, arguing that 'honeybees hurt the environment' by crowding out other kinds of insects and by hoarding honey which they don't need.[31]

It appears, however, that vegans and horror-film directors are being outgunned by the recent explosion of bee books for the layman in the past twenty years. William Longgood's *The Queen Must Die and Other Affairs of Bees and Men* (1985) is an informative personal memoir of bee-keeping, as is Sue Hubell's *A Book of Bees* (1988) and Rosemary Daryl Thomas's *Beeing: Life, Motherhood, and 180,000 Honeybees* (2002). As my own book was going to press, Hattie Ellis published *Sweetness and Light: The Mysterious History of the Honeybee* (2004), and the happily named Bee Wilson brought out *The Hive: The History of the Honeybee and Us* (2004). Since then, innumerable novels and self-help, inspirational and historical books have crowded the market. There is even a 'life coach' who has founded a system of self-help called 'The Bee Attitudes' – actually commandments – which include 'be part of something bigger than yourself', 'build for the future' and 'dance'.[32] The rehabilitation of the bee surfaced subtly and ironically in the 2004 National Spelling Bee in Washington, DC. The runner-up, a twelve-year-old boy from Colorado Springs, lost the title when he was unable to spell *schwärmerei*.

eleven

Retired Bee

Nine bean-rows will I have there, a hive for the honey bee,
And live alone in the bee-loud glade.
W. B. Yeats, 'The Lake Isle of Innisfree' (1888)[1]

S herlock Holmes retired to tend bees; in the Sussex Downs
he 'watched the little working gangs as once I watched the
criminal world of London'.[2] After his mountain exploits
were finished, Sir Edmund Hillary quit adventure for beekeeping in New Zealand. The vignette of the beekeeper or the observer
of bees leading the life of retirement and virtuous rural isolation is
a powerful recurrent theme from the Roman writers (Martial,
Virgil, Varro, Horace, Columella) to Thoreau at Walden Pond,
Yeats at Innisfree and Paul Theroux in Hawaii. The beekeeper, or
observer of bees, is traditionally apolitical and asocial, an interesting
pair of positions to set against the life of bees, which is hyper-social
and traditionally 'political'.

George MacKenzie, in praise of solitude, cites the life of Aristomarchus, who 'for fifty years employed himself in the observation
of Bees, and all that time found both new task and pleasure; and
never any could say that he had observed fully all that was to be
observed in floures, Anatomy, Astrology, or any of these Sciences
. . . and yet we complain that retirement . . . hath not employment or divertisement enough for us.'[3] Pliny had already reported
on Aristomarchus, as well as on the Sicilian historian Philistus

(430–356 BC), the so-called Wild Man, a lifelong beekeeper whose vocation may have assisted his writings on tyrants.[4] 'Happie is he, that from all Businesse cleere' can devote himself to an honest country task like beekeeping, who 'the prest honey in pure pots doth keepe'.[5]

At Walden Pond no natural phenomenon was too insignificant to interest Thoreau. An epic battle between red and black ants, narrated as a Homeric formicomachia, produces a meditation on power. Unusually for Thoreau, the bee could prompt less pleasant ruminations: the shape of the gluttonous bee-larva is retained in the adult insect form: 'the abdomen under the wings . . . still represents the larva', he notes, making the grubby appetitive stage latent in the aerial adult anatomy. 'The gross feeder', he concludes, 'is a man in the larva state; and there are whole nations in that condition, nations without fancy or imagination, whose vast abdomens betray them.'[6] This could be a description of the hive: a nation without fancy or imagination.

Paul Theroux, the novelist and travel writer, retired to the Hawaiian island of Oahu. Inspired by Sherlock Holmes, he too took up beekeeping, with 2 million bees in 80 hives. He has now entered the world of commercial honey production with a company called Oceania Ranch Pure Hawaiian Honey (established 1996), which nevertheless sells only to one restaurant in Honolulu. Theroux has said that writing and beekeeping are compatible with each other and with retirement; one of his novels features a Hawaiian beekeeper. This tradition thrives. A jeremiad against the trashiness of modern popular culture boasting the unvarnished title *Bollocks to Alton Towers* (2005) lists enjoyable and improving activities available to those wishing to avoid the ersatz purlieus of enormous amusement parks; one of these is the bee sanctuary at Porteath in Cornwall.[7]

In 2006, shortly after the first edition of this book was published, reports began to emerge of catastrophic and mysterious losses of entire hives in the USA. Typically, the beekeeper opened her hives one day to find them completely empty of worker bees – only the queen and a few attendants remained, with combs full of honey, pollen and brood. There was no sign of disease or attack or environmental crisis; there was no clue, either, as to where the missing bees had gone. This *Marie Celeste*-like discovery was called Colony Collapse Disorder (CCD), and although it had been known in small and manageable numbers for more than a century, it became widespread in the USA and Europe. In the years 2007–13, total CCD losses in some countries was as high as 50 per cent of all hives.[8] In the years since 2013, domestic bees have made something of a comeback, and CCD losses are significantly reduced, though not at normal pre-2006 annual rates. Although the phenomenon persists and is not fully understood, what is clear is that CCD is the result of the combined threats to bees produced by our environmental and agriculture management.[9] Aside from CCD among domestic bees, there has been a dangerous general decline in wild bee populations. For neither of these is there a convenient single culprit or simple cause: the stresses we place on bees are legion and include both mites and the miticides that treat them, agricultural pesticides (especially neonicotinoids), monoculture, malnutrition, climate change and mass transportation of bees by pollinator services.[10] Bees are especially vulnerable in their social organization: just as chaos ensues when one element fails in one of our complex human networks, so a single aberration in bee habitat or bee behaviour can wreak havoc on a whole species. One of the many constituents of CCD is the way that neonicotinoids appear to interfere with bee brains and specifically bee memory.[11] Sub-lethal exposure to this class of pesticide appears to make bees forget how to do their tasks, and when that happens, the colony dies. When bees die, our food sources are critically endangered.[12]

Bees stand for the difference between the life and death of our species and of our planet, as agricultural pollinators, as producers of food and light, as handmaidens of the wild vegetation without which our landscapes would be eroded, barren and empty of wildlife, and by whose efforts our soil is fertile. Africanized, bees are potentially able to affect the prosperity of our food production, and even the more benign strains can disrupt everyday life: in the spring of 2003 an overturned beetruck near Titusville, Florida, released millions of bees onto Interstate 95, the superhighway that runs down the east coast of the United States from Canada to the Keys, closing the road to traffic for six hours while officials rounded up the bees and scooped honey from the carriageway. If bees ever do retire from our landscapes, we may as well bid farewell to the earth as we know it. Linda Pastan's 'The Death of the Bee' imagines this horrifying and perhaps inevitable event:

> The biography of the bee
> is written in honey
> and is drawing to a close.
>
> Soon the buzzing
> plainchant of summer
> Will be silenced
> for good;
>
> the flowers, unkindled,
> will blaze
> one last time
> and go out.[13]

It is an inauspicious time for bees. The very behaviour that has made them such friends to man and so successful across the world now threatens them. Large-scale transportation of bees for migratory pollination spreads diseases like varroa and tracheal mites – themselves introduced by commercial imports to areas formerly free of them – and the genetic modification which has produced the Africanized honeybee was possible because bees consent to be tended and manipulated by human keepers. Wild and domestic bees are at risk from a range of commonly applied insecticides and miticides. An even more profound threat to bees is monoculture (large expanses of a single crop) and the disappearance of bee habitat, especially in densely developed countries.

It is tempting to think that the ancient tradition of the Civil Bee really can promote cooperative behaviour in other species, and there is one remarkable instance of interspecific symbiosis which seems almost to take a cue from bees. The honeyguide, an

Radar aerials attached to bees in 1996 allow scientists in Worcestershire
to track their movements.

The damaged bee on the left on Bernini's Fontana delle Api, Rome, was restored in 2015.

African bird which lives on beeswax and bee larvae, is so called because it leads Ghanaian honey hunters to the sites of wild bee-hives using a well-documented set of flight patterns and calls to indicate direction and distance. The humans open the hive and remove the honey, leaving the exposed combs and nursery cells for the birds, each profiting by the other's skill.[14] That this profit comes at the expense of virtuous bees whose own enterprise is a lesson in such partnerships is an irony only slightly more pronounced than the enlightened exploitation that beekeepers have practised for millennia. But joint enterprises between man and bee in the modern world are far grimmer than the search for wild honey or the comfortable hiving of bees. Almost as unbelievable as a bee movie, real bees have been trained to detect landmines, bombs and other explosives, as well as drugs and dead bodies. Not only do the water and nectar they retrieve contain traces of environmental contaminants taken up by vegetation, but bees can be trained, as dogs are, to seek certain scents, and may someday be used to scavenge harmful airborne microbial agents (such as might be released in a terrorist attacks).[15] They have become environmental messengers, the substances they gather in water, nectar, pollen and even blood gas analysed for ecological changes and health hazards.[16] As animal monitors of these various toxins and dangers, bees are likely to perish in the very act of bringing us the dire tidings of our own terrible technologies. These deadly tasks were unimagined, of course, by the early fabricators of bee legend, when the bee was a signature of simplicity, selflessness, innocence and peace. In the increasingly melancholy history of our own species, whose arts of life are being turned into the arts of death, the bee gravely insists by example that we look beyond ourselves.

When bees retire from society, it is to die. The span of a bee's life is poignantly brief – it cannot live through the whole of the brood-rearing season, or the full honey flow of summer. Only the overwintering bees ever know the difference between one season and the next, between warm and cold air, and most of them experience it only in the difference between the balmy days of summer and the intensely crowded ball of bees who huddle together in winter for warmth in the hive. One bee is a frail, momentary being; the hive alone possesses longevity.

But if real bees are mortal, the bees of art and legend ought to be imperishable, with no imperious mortality to make spoil of their beauty. In July 2004, as this book was nearing completion, vandals smashed one of the beautiful stone bees carved by Bernini for the Fontana delle Api in Rome. In life, it is true, one bee is no bee, but the defacement of the graceful sculpted fountain by so much as a single bee damaged the public work of art and by extension the polity of Rome. It is an ironic (and probably unintended) comment on the 'civility' of modern life that there can be no other animal image whose destruction carries such specific symbolic messages about the way we live now. Such reckless acts of damage are completely unknown to bees, and their own art survives because untold thousands and millions cooperate in keeping it sound and perfect. The Bernini fountain, stranded in the twenty-first century at what is now a busy urban intersection, surrounded (as real bees almost never are) by the roar of traffic, assaulted by exhaust fumes and mired in litter, has serenely survived intact for four centuries, its stone bees eternally climbing its surface as if making good the precious comb. That one bee is now a broken one is heartbreaking evidence – evidence which would be quite lost on real bees – of our world, our past, our culture, how we got from wherever we began to the here and now.

Timeline of the Bee

Primitive solitary bee species originate in southern Asia	Social bee species produce honey	Valencia drawings of honey-hunting	Earliest records of human consumption of honey	Sumerians use honey for skin ulcers

Richard Remnant in *A Discourse or Historie of Bees* shows that the workers are female	Tomb of Merovingian King Childeric I (*d*. 481) is excavated at Tournai, yielding 300 golden bees	Swammerdam, the Dutch microscopist, produces full anatomical drawings of the queen, the worker and the drone	George Wheler discovers and describes the Greek hive, forerunner of the movable-frame modern hive	Realization that bees make honey and do not gather it from flowers

Mormons reach Utah and name it 'Deseret', 'land of the honeybee'	L. L. Langstroth of Philadelphia constructs the first completely movable-frame hive	Bulgarian soldiers in the Balkan war resort to honey to dress wounds when their conventional medicines run short	Lenin issues the decree for the protection of beekeeping	Joseph Beuys makes the first of his bee-related sculptures

2,400 years	c. 1st AD:	300–600	1538	1586	1625
Beekeeping in Egypt	Virgil's *Georgics* establish many persistent ideas about the social organization of bees	Picts manufacture honey ale	Spanish import the first hived European honeybees to South America	First suggestion that the head bee is female and lays all the eggs	Accademia Lincei performs first microscopic observations of bee and produces detailed drawings

1744	1750	1788	1790s	1820s–30s
Beeswax is shown to be produced by young bees	Pollen is recognized as the male seed of the flower; honeybees are observed to be flower-specific	Bee dances are observed among foraging workers	Bee and hive images are adopted by the propagandists of the French Republic	'Never Kill a Bee' movement

1949	1953	1957	1965	2000
International Bee Research Association (IBRA) founded in England	Karl von Frisch, a German ethologist, explains apian communication in *The Dancing Bees*, for which he wins the Nobel Prize in 1973	Africanized European honeybees escape into the Brazilian rainforest; the cult of the 'killer bee' begins	Honey is one-and-a-half times as expensive as sugar in the United States, and up to six times more expensive in Germany	Mayor of Moscow cultivates bees and advertises himself as a man of the people

References

1 THE REASONS FOR BEES

1 A. A. Milne, 'In Which We Are Introduced to Winnie-the-Pooh and Some Bees, and the Stories Begin', *Winnie-the-Pooh* (London, 1926), p. 10.

2 See www.vegetus.org/honey/honey.htm, a radical vegan website.

3 Thomas Hobbes, *Leviathan* (Cambridge, 1991), chapter 17, p. 119.

4 Arthur Conan Doyle, 'His Last Bow', in *The Annotated Sherlock Holmes*, ed. William S. Baring-Gould (New York, 1960), II, p. 803.

5 George MacKenzie, *A Moral Essay Preferring Solitude to Publick Employment* (London, 1665), p. 80.

6 Henry David Thoreau, *Journal III* (13 February 1852), in *Thoreau's Writings*, ed. Bradford Torrey (Boston, 1906), IX, p. 299.

7 James Fenimore Cooper, *The Oak Openings, or The Bee-Hunter* (New York, 1848), p. 19.

8 Claude Lévi-Strauss, *From Honey to Ashes: Introduction to a Science of Mythology*, II, trans. John and Doreen Weightman (New York, 1973), pp. 28, 35, 55, 289.

9 Pausanias, *Description of Greece*, trans. W.H.S. Jones and H. A. Ormerod (Cambridge, MA, 1965–6), book IX, chapter 23, line 2.

10 Hilda M. Ransome, *The Sacred Bee in Ancient Times and Folklore* [1937] (Bridgwater, 1986), p. 105.

11 Herman Melville, *Moby-Dick* (1851, Harmondsworth, 1972), chap. 78, p. 326.

12 Thomas Pecke, *Parnassi Puerperium* (London, 1659), p. 156.

13 Qu'ran, 47: 17, 18.

14 Sue Monk Kidd, *The Secret Life of Bees* (New York, 2002), p. 137.

15 Samuel Purchas, *A Treatise of Politicall Flying-insects* (London, 1657), p. 16.

16 Jacques Vanière, *The Bees. A Poem*, trans. Arthur Murphy (London, 1799), p. 5.

17 Maurice Maeterlinck, *The Life of the Bee*, trans. Alfred Sutro (New York, 1924), p. 30.

18 Osip Mandelstam, 'Take from my palms', in *Selected Poems: A Necklace of Bees*, trans. Maria Enzensberger (London, 1992), p. 22.

19 Osip Mandelstam, 'Whoever finds a horseshoe' (number 136), in *The Complete Poetry of Osip Emilevich Mandelstam*, trans. Burton Raffel and Alla Burago (Albany, NY, 1973). Bees are frequently found in Mandelstam's work.

2 BIOLOGICAL BEE

1 Maurice Maeterlinck, *The Life of the Bee*, trans. Alfred Sutro (New York, 1924), p. 57.

2 All ant-species and many wasp-species are social.

3 Eva Crane, *Bees and Beekeeping: Science, Practice and World Resources* (Oxford, 1990), p. 7.

4 See Rex Boys's excellent account of the apidictor on www.beedata.com.

5 Joseph Hall, 'Upon Bees Fighting', *Occasional Meditations* (London, 1630), p. 150.

6 See ananova.com.

7 Karl von Frisch, *The Dancing Bee: An Account of the Life and Senses of the Honey Bee*, trans. Dora Lane (New York, 1955), pp. 101–33. The dances of bees are discussed in chapter 7.

1 Moses Rusden, *A Further Discovery of Bees* (London, 1679), p. 8.

2 Hilda M. Ransome, *The Sacred Bee in Ancient Times and Folklore* (Bridgwater, 1986), p. 55.

3 Pliny, *Historia Naturalis*, trans. H. Rackham (London and Cambridge, MA, 1967), III, p. 451.

4 On Chinese beekeeping before 1500 see Ransome, *Sacred Bee*, pp. 52–4.

5 Samuel Purchas, *A Treatise of Politicall Flying-insects* (London, 1657), p. 140.

6 S. Buchmann and G. Nabham, 'The Pollination Crisis: The Plight of the Honey Bee and the Decline of other Pollinators Imperils Future Harvests', *The Sciences*, 36 (4), (1997), pp. 22–8.

7 William Cotton, *A Short and Simple Letter to Cottagers, from a Conservative Bee-Keeper* (London, 1838), p. 4.

8 *Observations and Notes* in *The Works of Sir Thomas Browne*, ed. Geoffrey Keynes (Chicago, 1964), III, p. 247.

9 Rusden, *A Further Discovery of Bees*, p. 38.

10 Ibid., p. 9.

11 John Evelyn, *Diary* (London, 1950), 13 July 1654, p. 295. Samuel Hartlib, *The Reformed Commonwealth of Bees* (London, 1655), pp. 45, 50–52.

12 Samuel Pepys, *Diary* (Ware, 1997), 5 May 1665, p. 329.

13 John Evelyn, *Kalendarium Hortense, or, the Gardener's Almanac* (London, 1664), p. 71.

14 Robert Plot, *The Natural History of Oxfordshire* (London, 1677), p. 263; Nehemiah Grew, *Musæum Regalis Societatis* (London, 1685), p. 371.

15 The figures are from the American National Honey Board (www.nhb.org).

16 Emily Dickinson, 'The pedigree of honey', in *The Complete Poems of Emily Dickinson*, ed. Thomas H. Johnson (London, 1970), pp. 668–9.

4 POLITICAL BEE

1 *The Divine Weeks and Works of Guillaume de Saluste du Bartas*, trans. Joshua Sylvester, ed. Susan Snyder (Oxford, 1979), I, ll. 919–20.

2 Jacques Vanière, *The Bees. A Poem*, trans. Arthur Murphy (London, 1799), p. 6.

3 Thomas Moffett, *Insectorum sive minimorum animalium theatrum*, in Edward Topsell, *The History of Fourfooted Beasts and Serpents . . . whereunto is now added The Theater of Insects* (London, 1658), p. 894.

4 Thomas Adams, *The Happiness of the Church* (London, 1666), p. 204. See also Stephen Batman (or Bateman), *Batman upon Bartholomew* (London, 1582), chap. 4.

5 Hesiod, *Works and Days* (Harmondsworth, 1985), p. 68.

6 Varro, *Rerum Rusticarum*, trans. W. D. Hooper and H. B. Ash (Cambridge, MA, 1934), book III, section 15, p. 503.

7 John Gay, 'The Degenerate Bees', in *Fables* (London, 1795), p. 174.

8 Charles Butler, *The Feminine Monarchie* (London, 1609), p. B6v.

9 John Adams, *An Essay Concerning Self-murther* (London, 1700), p. 95.

10 Virgil, *Georgics*, trans. John Dryden (London, 1697), p. 229.

11 Ibid., p. 217.

12 Frances Trollope, *The Domestic Manners of the Americans* [1832], ed. Richard Mullen (Oxford, 1984), p. 36.

13 Henry David Thoreau, *Journal IV* (30 September 1852) in *Thoreau's Writings*, ed. Bradford Torrey (Boston, 1906), p. 373.

14 Samuel Purchas, *A Treatise of Politicall Flying-insects* (London, 1657), p. 17.

15 Seneca, 'De Clementia', in *Seneca's Morals Extracted in Three Books*, trans. Roger L'Estrange (London, 1679), pp. 139–40; and *Epistulae*

    ad Lucilium, trans. Richard M. Gunmere (Cambridge, MA, 1917),
    II, 84.3.b.

16 Godfrey Goodman, *The Fall of Man; or, The Corruption of Nature*
    (London, 1616), p. 100.

17 William Allen, *A Conference About the Next Succession* (London, 1595),
    p. 205.

18 William Shakespeare, *Henry V* (London, 1969), I.ii.187–203.

19 Moffett, *Insectorum,* p. 893.

20 Ibid., pp. 892–3.

21 Purchas, *Treatise*, pp. 3–4. The etymology of 'bee' was creatively estab-
    lished in various languages. The English word 'bee' comes from
    Anglo-Saxon *bēo*, bee.

22 Moffett, *Insectorum*, p. 891.

23 Butler, *Feminine Monarchie*, p. a3v.

24 Moses Rusden, *A Further Discovery of Bees* (London, 1679),
    p. A2[v], 1.

25 Butler, *Feminine Monarchie*, p. a3v.

26 Purchas, *Treatise*, p. 17.

27 Robert Hooke, *Micrographia* (London, 1665), p. 163.

28 John Levett, *The Ordering of Bees; or, The True History of Managing
    Them* (London, 1634), p. 34.

29 Ibid., p. 68.

30 Hilda M. Ransome, *The Sacred Bee in Ancient Times and Folklore*
    (Bridgwater, 1986), p. 234.

31 Les Murray, 'The Swarm', in *Collected Poems* (Manchester, 1991), p. 151.

32 Samuel Hartlib, *The Reformed Commonwealth of Bees* (London, 1655),
    p. 4.

33 Columella, *De Rustica*, trans. E. S. Forster and Edward H. Heffner
    (Cambridge, MA, 1954), II, p. 483.

34 Moffett, *Insectorum*, p. 895.

35 Columella, *De Rustica*, p. 483.

36 Butler, *Feminine Monarchie*, pp. a7v, b5v.

37 Frederic Tubach, *Index Exemplorum: A Handbook of Medieval Religious Tales* (Helsinki, 1969), p. 47 (no. 545).

38 Robert Herrick, 'The Wounded Cupid' [1648], in *The Poetical Works of Robert Herrick* (Oxford, 1956), p. 50.

39 Filips van Marnix, *De Roomsche Byen-korf* [1569], trans. John Still (London, 1579).

40 Virgil, *Georgics*, pp. 223, 221.

41 Richard Day, *The Parliament of Bees* (London, 1697), p. 2.

42 Isaac Watts, 'Against Idleness and Mischief', in *Works* (London, 1810), IV, p. 399.

43 Gay, 'The Degenerate Bees', *Fables*, p. 174.

44 Emily Dickinson, 'Partake as doth the bee', in *Complete Poems*, ed. T. H. Johnson (London, 1975), p. 462 (no. 994).

45 François Mitterrand, *The Wheat and the Chaff* (includes *L'abeille et l'architecte*) (London, 1982).

46 Vanière, *The Bees*, pp. xi, 27, 41.

47 Mary Alcock, 'The Hive of Bees: A Fable, Written December, 1792', in *Poems* (London, 1799), pp. 25–30.

48 Anon., 'The Secret of the Bees', in *Liberty Lyrics*, ed. Louisa S. Bevington (London, 1895), p. 6.

49 Charles E. Waterman, *Apiatia: Little Essays on Honey-Makers* (Medina, OH, 1933), p. 14.

50 Moffett, *Insectorum*, p. 894.

51 Waterman, *Apiatia*, p. 12.

52 Robert Graves, 'Secession of the Drones', in *Complete Poems* (Manchester, 1997), II, pp. 192–3.

53 Henri Cole, 'The Lost Bee', *American Poetry Review*, 33 (2004), p. 40.

1 H. Hawkins, *Parthenia Sacra* (London, 1633), p. 74.

2 Qu'ran, 16:68–9.

3 Ovid, *Metamorphoses*, trans. Rolfe Humphries (Bloomington, IN, 1955),
book i, ll. 110–11.

4 Dante, *Paradiso*, trans. Laurence Binyon (London, 1979), Canto 31,
lines 4–24.

5 William Wordsworth, 'Vernal Ode', v, ll. 124–8, in *Poetical Works*,
ed. T. Hutchinson and E. de Selincourt (Oxford, 1936), p. 181.

6 Hawkins, *Parthenia Sacra*, p. 71.

7 Virgil, *Georgics*, trans. John Dryden (London, 1697), p. 225.

8 Hawkins, *Parthenia Sacra*, p. 74.

9 George Gilpin, *The Beehive of the Romish Church* (1579), quoted in
Hilda M. Ransome, *The Sacred Bee in Ancient Times and Folklore*
(Bridgwater, 1986), p. 148.

10 Eva Crane, *A Book of Honey* (Oxford, 1980), p. 138.

11 Psalms 81:16.

12 Luke 24:39–43.

13 This metaphor was widely and richly deployed in relation to the
medieval monastic orders.

14 Ralph Austen, *The Spirituall Use of an Orchard* (London, 1653),
p. [t2v].

15 'The Bee and the Stork' (from the Thornton ms, fol. 194, Lincoln
Cathedral Library), reprinted in *The English Writings of Richard Rolle*,
ed. Hope Emily Allen (Oxford, 1931), pp. 54–5.

16 Henry Ellison, 'Lose Not Time', in *Stones from the Quarry*
(London, 1875); see also his 'The Poetical Hive' and 'Hint to Poets'
in the same collection.

17 Quoted in Eudo C. Mason, *Rilke* (Edinburgh and London, 1963),
pp. 89–90.

18 Gilpin, quoted in Ransome, *Sacred Bee*, p. 147.

19 Thomas Moffett, *Insectorum sive minimorum animalium theatrum*, in Edward Topsell, *The History of Fourfooted Beasts and Serpents . . . whereunto is now added The Theater of Insects* (London, 1658), p. 96.

20 Emanuele Tesauro, *Il Cannochiale Aristotelico* (Rome, 1664), p. 94.

21 Samuel Purchas, *A Treatise of Politicall Flying-insects* (London, 1657), p. 42.

22 Purchas, *Treatise*, p. 19.

23 Charles Butler, *The Feminine Monarchie* (London, 1609), pp. b2v–b3R.

24 R. S. Hawker, 'The Legend of the Hive', in *Poetical Works* (London, 1899), pp. 105–8.

25 Hawkins, *Parthenia Sacra*, p. 70.

26 George Wither, *The Schollers Purgatory Discovered in the Stationers Common-wealth* (London, 1624), p. 5.

27 Walter Raleigh, 'The History of the World', in *The Works of Sir Walter Raleigh, Kt* (New York, 1929), II, p. xvi.

28 Butler, *Feminine Monarchie*, p. a1v.

29 Moffett, *Insectorum*, p. 891.

30 Ibid.

31 Moses Rusden, *A Further Discovery of Bees* (London, 1679), p. [a8v].

32 James Boswell, *An Account of Corsica* (London, 1768), p. 280.

33 Anne Hughes, *Diary of a Farmer's Wife, 1796–1797* (London, 1980), p. 78.

34 William Cotton, *A Short and Simple Letter to Cottagers, from a Conservative Bee-Keeper* (London, 1838), p. 2.

35 William Cotton, *My Bee Book* (London, 1842), p. cxl.

36 Diana Hartog, *Polite to Bees: A Bestiary* (Toronto, 1992), p. 54.

37 Purchas, *Treatise*, p. 113.

38 Joseph Hall, 'Upon Bees Fighting', in *Occasional Meditations* (London, 1630), pp. 148–9.

39 A. I. Root, *The ABC and XYZ of Bee Culture* (Medina, OH, 1908), p. 362.

40 Judges 14:5–14.

41 Virgil, *Georgics*, ll. 452–8.

42 Ovid, *Metamorphoses*, XV, ll. 365ff.

43 Purchas, *Treatise*, p. 44, paraphrasing Aristotle, *De generatione animalium*, III.10.

44 Purchas, *Treatise*, p. 46.

45 Godfrey Goodman, *The Fall of Man; or, The Corruption of Nature* (London, 1616), p. 19.

46 Edward G. Ruestow, *The Microscope in the Dutch Republic: The Shaping of Discovery* (Cambridge, 1996), p. 201.

47 John Greenleaf Whittier, 'The Hive at Gettysburg', in *Poetical Works* (Boston, 1894), III, pp. 263–4.

6 UTILE BEE

1 William Cotton, *A Short and Simple Letter to Cottagers, from a Conservative Bee-Keeper* (London, 1838), p. 3.

2 *Desert Island Discs*, BBC Radio 4, broadcast of 19 May 2002.

3 Joe Traynor, *Honey, the Gourmet Medicine* (Bakersfield, CA, 2002), p. 63.

4 Peter Molan, 'The Anti-Bacterial Activity of Honey, Part I', *Bee World*, 73 (1992), pp. 5–28, and Eva Crane, *Bees and Beekeeping: Science, Practice and World Resources* (Oxford, 1990), pp. 426–7.

5 Traynor, *Honey*, pp. 8–12.

6 Ibid., p. 13.

7 John Aubrey, 'Adversaria Physica', in *Three Prose Works*, ed. John Buchanan-Brown (Carbondale, IL, 1972), pp. 345, 353.

8 *The Catholic Directory, 1943* (London, 1943), p. 111.

9 A. I. Root, *The ABC and XYZ of Bee Culture* (Medina, OH, 1908), pp. 331–2.

10 See John R. Davis, *The Great Exhibition* (Stroud, 1999), p. 143.

11 Bryan Acton and Peter Duncan, *Making Mead* (Ann Arbor, MI, 1984), n.p.

12 'The Prairies', in *American Poetry*, ed. John Hollander (New York, 1993), I, pp. 162–5.

7 AESTHETIC BEE

1 Geffrey Whitney, *A Choice of Emblems* (London, 1586), p. 200.

2 Maurice Maeterlinck, *The Life of the Bee*, trans. Alfred Sutro (New York, 1924), pp. 406–7.

3 Wordsworth, 'Vernal Ode', IV, ll. 107–8, in *Poetical Works*, ed. T. Hutchinson and E. de Selincourt (Oxford, 1936).

4 William A. McClung, *The Architecture of Paradise: Survivals of Eden and Jerusalem* (Berkeley, CA, 1983), p. 118.

5 Thomas Browne, *The Garden of Cyrus*, in *Works*, ed. Geoffrey Keynes (Chicago, 1964), III, p. 102.

6 Maeterlinck, *Life of the Bee*, p. 189.

7 Christopher Smart, 'The Blockhead and the Beehive', in *Poems* (London, 1791), pp. 26–30.

8 A. I. Root, *The ABC and XYZ of Bee Culture* (Medina, OH, 1908), pp. 172–8.

9 Henry Ellison, 'The Poetical Hive', in *Stones from the Quarry* (London, 1875), n.p.

10 Quoted in François Mitterrand, *The Wheat and the Chaff* (London, 1982), epigraph.

11 For a detailed study of the bee and the beehive motif in Gaudí's work, see Juan Antonio Ramirez, *The Beehive Metaphor: From Gaudí to Le Corbusier* (London, 2000).

12 See Ramirez, *Beehive Metaphor*, p. 128.

13 Caroline Tisdall, *Joseph Beuys* (London, 1979), p. 44.

14 Karl von Frisch, *The Dancing Bee: An Account of the Life and Senses of the Honey Bee*, trans. Dora Lane (New York, 1955), pp. 91–133.

15 Wordsworth, 'Vernal Ode', IV, Bryant's 'Summer Wind' and Emerson's 'The Humble-Bee' can be found in *American Poetry*, ed. John Hollander (New York, 1993), I, p. 146 (Bryant) and p. 272 (Emerson).

16 Charles Horn, *The Bee-Hive* (London, 1811); James Elliott, *The Bee* (London, 1825); William Hawes, *The Bee* (London, 1836); Julia Woolf and Agnes Trevor, *The Bee and the Rose* (London, 1877).

17 Walt Whitman, 'Bumble Bees', from *Specimen Days*, reprinted in *Walt Whitman: The Complete Poetry and Collected Prose* (New York, 1982), pp. 783–6.

18 Charles Butler, *The Feminine Monarchie* (2nd edn, London, 1623), chap. 5, pp. K4V-L1R.

19 www.beedata.com.

20 'It was a time when silly bees could speak', Song 18 in John Dowland, *The Third and Last Booke of Songs or Aires* (London, 1603), p. L1R.

8 FOLKLORIC BEE

1 Columella, *De Rustica*, trans. E. S. Forster and Edward H. Heffner (Cambridge, MA, 1954), II, p. 429.

2 Gertrude Jones, *Dictionary of Mythology, Folklore, and Symbols* (New York, 1962), I, p. 193.

3 Ovid, *Fasti*, trans. James Frazer (Cambridge, MA, 1931), III, ll. 736–63.

4 William Combe, *Doctor Syntax in Search of Consolation* (London, 1820), collected in *Doctor Syntax's Three Tours* (London, 1869), p. 209.

5 John Greenleaf Whittier, 'Telling the Bees' [1860], in *American Poetry*, ed. John Hollander (New York, 1993), I, pp. 468–70.

6 Frederic Tubach, *Index Exemplorum: A Handbook of Medieval Religious Tales* (Helsinki, 1969), no. 550.

7 Eva Crane, *A Book of Honey* (Oxford, 1980), p. 134.

8 G. Henderson, *Folklore of the Northern Counties* (1879), cited in Hilda M. Ransome, *The Sacred Bee in Ancient Times and Folklore* (Bridgwater, 1986), p. 229.

9 John Worlidge, *Apiarium* (London, 1676), 'To the Reader', p. [a3v]. Interested readers are directed to *The Bees*, a modern Aristophanic

pastiche by F. Lepper in celebration of his *alma mater*, the so-called College of Bees.

10 Antony á Wood, 'Fasti Oxoniensis ', in *Athenae Oxoniensis* (London, 1691), II, p. 693.

11 Tacitus, *Annals*, trans. John Jackson (Cambridge, MA, 1970), IV, book XII, chap. LXIV.

12 Livy, *History of Rome*, trans. Frank G. Moore (Cambridge, MA, 1963), VII, book XXVII, chap. XIII.

13 Emily Dickinson, 'The murmuring of bees has ceased', in *The Complete Poems of Emily Dickinson*, ed. Thomas H. Johnson (London, 1970), p. 502 (no. 1115).

14 *The Book of Mormon*, Ether 2:3.

15 Samuel Purchas, *A Treatise of Politicall Flying-insects* (London, 1657), p. 121.

16 Ransome, *Sacred Bee*, pp. 181–2.

17 Virgil, *Georgics*, trans. John Dryden (London, 1697), l. 286; Pliny, *Historia Naturalis*, 10 vols, trans. H. Rackham (London and Cambridge, MA, 1967), XI, p. 447; Nehemiah Grew, *Musæum Regalis Societatis* (London, 1685), p. 154.

18 Pliny, *Historia Naturalis*, XI, iv–xiii, p. 439.

19 Purchas, *Treatise*, p. 120.

20 Jonston, *An History of the Wonderful Things of Nature* (London, 1657), p. 244.

21 Ibid., p. 245; Grew, *Musæum*, p. 155.

22 Columella, *De Rustica*, II, p. 475; Varro, *Rerum Rusticarum*, trans. W. D. Hooper and H. B. Ash (Cambridge, MA, 1934), p. 521.

23 William Cotton, *My Bee Book* (London, 1842), p. 231.

24 Henry Thoreau, *Journal III*, 30 September 1852, in *Thoreau's Writings*, ed. Bradford Torrey (Boston, 1906), IV, p. 375.

25 Gustave Aimard, *The Bee-Hunters* (London, 1864), p. 44.

9 PLAYFUL BEE

1 Richard Klein, *Eat Fat* (London, 1997), pp. 185–6.

2 Quoted by Walt Whitman, 'Bumble-Bees', *Specimen Days*, reprinted in *Walt Whitman: The Complete Poetry and Collected Prose* (New York, 1982), pp. 785–6.

3 Ibid.

4 Emily Dickinson, 'I taste a liquor never brewed', in *Complete Poems*, ed. Thomas H. Johnson (London, 1975), p. 98 (no. 214).

5 Robert Frankum, *The Bee and the Wasp: A Fable* (London, 1832).

6 'Bee Song', in Kenneth Blain, *Songs and Monologues Performed by Arthur Askey*, gramophone record, London, 1947.

7 W. S. Gilbert, 'The Independent Bee', in *Bab Ballads* (London, 1898), pp. 536–8.

8 Edward Lear, *A Book of Nonsense* (London, 1861), limerick 10.

9 Robert R. Kirk, 'Bees', in *Poetry: Its Appreciation and Enjoyment*, ed. Louis Untermeyer and Carter Davison (New York, 1934), p. 318.

10 www.filmforce.ign.com/articles. I resist including the nonsensical 'Eric the Half-a-Bee' song by Monty Python.

10 BEE MOVIE

1 The Bobs, 'Killer Bees', in *Songs for Tomorrow Morning*, Rhino Records, 1988.

2 See Paul Fussell, *The Rhetorical World of Augustan Humanism* (Oxford, 1965), pp. 233–4, quoting Pope's *The Dunciad*.

3 Edmund Burke, *Letter to a Noble Lord* (London, 1795), pp. 79–80.

4 See Jonathan Bate, *The Romantic Ecologists* (London, 1991), pp. 79–80.

5 William Wordsworth, *The Excursion*, VIII, ll. 329–30, in *Poetical Works*, ed. T. Hutchinson and E. de Selincourt (Oxford, 1936).

6 John Ruskin, 'The Nature of Gothic', in *The Stones of Venice*, ed. J. G. Links (London, 1960), pp. 164–5.

7 William Blake, *Jerusalem: The Emanation of the Giant Albion* (1804), reprinted in *The Poems*, ed. W. H. Stevenson and David H. Erdman (London, 1971), l. 16.

8 Thomas Carlyle, letter to Alex Carlyle, quoted in Humphrey Jennings, *Pandæmonium* (London, 1985), p. 164.

9 Samuel Taylor Coleridge, *Biographia Literaria* (Princeton, NJ, 1984), book 1, chap. 2.

10 Eric McLuhan, quoted in T. Curtis Hayward, *Bees of the Invisible: Creative Play and Divine Possession* (London: The Guild of Pastoral Psychology, no. 206, n.d. [*c.* 1982]), p. 9.

11 Edward Paley, 'Fable of the Bee-Hive', in *Reasons for Contentment Addressed to the Labouring Part of the British Public* (London, 1831), pp. 22–4.

12 David Wojahn, 'The Hivekeepers', in *Late Empire* (Pittsburgh, 1994), pp. 12–14.

13 A. I. Root, *The ABC and XYZ of Bee Culture* (Medina, OH, 1908), p. 13.

14 Hart Crane, 'The Hive', in *The Complete Poems and Selected Letters and Prose* (Garden City, NJ, 1986), p. 127.

15 Elias Canetti, *Crowds and Power*, trans. Carol Stewart (London, 1962), pp. 29–30.

16 Sir John Lubbock, *Ants, Bees and Wasps* [1881] (London, 1915), p. 284.

17 Lubbock, *Ants, Bees and Wasps*, p. 281, quoting Langstroth's *Treatise on the Honey-Bee* (1876).

18 Lubbock, *Ants, Bees and Wasps*, p. 285.

19 Maurice Maeterlinck, *The Life of the Bee*, trans. Alfred Sutro (New York, 1924), pp. 44, 89.

20 Ibid., p. 66.

21 Ibid., p. 32.

22 Ibid., p. 47.

23 Ibid., p. 50.

24 Rudolf Steiner, *Bees*, trans. Thomas Brantz (Hudson, NY, 1998), pp. 4–8.

25 A complete account of the Africanized bee is to be found in Mark Winston, *Killer Bees: The Africanized Honey Bee in the Americas* (Cambridge, MA, 1992).

26 I. Khalifman, *Bees* (Moscow, 1953), pp. 12, 19–21.

27 I am indebted to the informative and witty Jabootu Nation bad movie site (www.jabootu.com) for additional insights into the badness of bee movies.

28 www.imdb.com.

29 Further bee-related films include the Indian *Bees* (1991); *Bee Season* (2005), about a therapeutic spelling bee; *Die Bumble Bees* (1982), a fantasy; *Bubble Bee* (1949), featuring Donald Duck and a pesky bee arguing about a piece of bubble gum; *The Bee-Deviled Bruin* (1949), a Chuck Jones cartoon starring Stan Freberg as the voice of Junyer Bear; *Bees in Paradise* (1944), a musical comedy about castaways on a desert island dominated by women who worship bees and kill their husbands after two months of marriage; *Honey Bee* (1920), an office melodrama; and *Bees in His Bonnet* (1918), a documentary about daily life in Britain.

30 Thomas McMahon, *McKay's Bees* (London, 1979), p. 1.

31 See www.vegetus.org.

32 ASKBARB@aol.com.

11 RETIRED BEE

1 W. B. Yeats, 'The Lake Isle of Innisfree', in *Collected Poems* (London, 1950), p. 44.

2 Arthur Conan Doyle, 'His Last Bow', in *The Annotated Sherlock Holmes*, ed. William S. Baring-Gould (New York, 1960), II, p. 804.

3 George MacKenzie, *A Moral Essay Preferring Solitude to Publick Employment* (London, 1665), p. 80.

4 Pliny, *Historia Naturalis*, trans. H. Rackham (London and Cambridge, MA, 1967), XI, p. 445.

5 Ben Jonson, translating Horace's *Epode* II ('*Beatus ille*'), in Jonson's *Poems*, ed. Ian Donaldson (Oxford, 1975), pp. 274–6.

6 Henry David Thoreau, *Walden*, ed. J. Lyndon Stanley (Princeton, NJ, 1971), p. 215.

7 Jason Hazeley, et al., *Bollocks to Alton Towers* (London, 2005), pp. 33–5.

8 Bryan Walsh, 'The Plight of the Honeybee', cover story, *Time*, 15 May 2014.

9 The United States Department of Agriculture's discussion of bee stressors ('Honeybees and Colony Collapse Disorder: Research Directions' (www.ars.usda.gov/News/docs.htm?docid=15572#research).

10 Francis Ratnieks and Norman Carreck, 'Clarity on Honey Bee Collapse?', *Science* 8:327:5962 (2010), pp. 152–3.

11 For example, Mary J. Palmer, Christopher Moffat, Nastja Saranzewa, Jenni Harvey, Geraldine A. Wright, and Christopher N. Connolly, 'Cholinergic pesticides cause mushroom body neronal inactivation in honeybees', *Nature Communications*, 4 (2013) (www.nature.com/ncomms/journal/v4/n3/full/ncomms2648.html); Jennifer Hopwood et al., *Are Neonicotinoids Killing Bees? A Review of Research into the Effects of Neonicotinoid Insecticides on Bees, with Recommendations for Action* (Portland, OR, 2012) (http://ento.psu.edu/publications/are-neonicotinoids-killing-bees); Sally M. Williamson et al., 'Acute Exposure to a Sublethal Dose of Imidacloprid and Comaphos Enhances Olfactory Learning and Memory in the Honeybee *Apis melifera*', *Invertebrate Neuroscience*, 13 (2013), pp. 63–70; A. Decourtye et al., 'Imidacloprid Impairs Memory and Brain Metabolism in the Honeybee (*Apis mellifera L.*)', *Pesticide Biochemistry and Physiology*, 78 (2004), pp. 83–92.

12 In the UK, honeybee pollination is essential for at least 70 crops and accounts for £200 million in the national economy (British Beekeepers Association: www.bbka.org.uk); in the USA the figure is $19.2 billion; and all bee species together account for $29 billion in farm revenues from 58 plant species (*Cornell Chronicle*, 22 May 2012: www.news.cornell.edu).

13 Linda Pastan, 'The Death of the Bee', *Kenyon Review*, 20 (1998), p. 73.

14 See A. A. Isack and H.-U. Reyer, 'Honeyguides and Honey Gatherers: Interspecific Communication in a Symbiotic Relationship', *Science*, 243 (10 March 1989), pp. 1343–6.

15 Jerry J. Bromenshenk, 'Can Honey Bees Assist in Area Reduction and Landmine Detection?', *Journal of Mine Action*, VII/3 (2003), pp. 380–89.

16 United States Environmental Protection Agency report (January 1999): www.epa.gov.

Bibliography

Acton, Bryan, and Peter Duncan, *Making Mead* (Ann Arbor, MI, 1984)

Aimard, Gustave, *The Bee-Hunters* (London, 1864)

Alcock, Mary, 'The Hive of Bees: A Fable, Written December, 1792',
in *Poems* (London, 1799)

Allen, William, *A Conference about the Next Succession* (London, 1595)

Anon., 'The Secret of the Bees', in *Liberty Lyrics*, ed. Louisa S. Bevington
(London, 1895)

Aubrey, John, *Adversaria Physica* in *Three Prose Works*, ed. John Buchanan-
Brown (Carbondale, IL, 1972)

Austen, Ralph, *The Spirituall Use of an Orchard* (London, 1653)

Bate, Jonathan, *The Romantic Ecologists* (London, 1991)

Bromenshenk, Jerry J., 'Can Bees Assist in Area Reduction and Landmine
Detection?', *Journal of Mine Action*, VII/3 (2003), pp. 380–89
(Proceedings of the First International Joint Conference on Point
Detection for Chemical and Biological Defense)

Browne, Thomas, *The Works of Sir Thomas Browne*, 4 vols, ed. Geoffrey
Keynes, 2nd edn (Chicago, 1964)

Buchmann, S., and G. Nabham, 'The Pollination Crisis: The Plight
of the Honey Bee and the Decline of other Pollinators Imperils Future
Harvests', *The Sciences*, 36(4) (1997), pp. 182–3

Burke, Edmund, *Letter to a Noble Lord* (London, 1795)

Butler, Charles, *The Feminine Monarchie* (London, 1609; 2nd edn 1623)

Canetti, Elias, *Crowds and Power*, trans. Carol Stewart (London, 1962)

Cole, Henri, 'The Lost Bee', *American Poetry Review*, 33 (2004), p. 40

Coleridge, Samuel Taylor, *Biographia Literaria* (Princeton, NJ, 1984)

Columella, *De Rustica*, 3 vols, trans. E. S. Forster and Edward H. Heffner
(Cambridge, MA, 1954)

Conan Doyle, Arthur, 'His Last Bow', in *The Annotated Sherlock Holmes*,
2 vols, ed. William S. Baring-Gould (New York, 1960), II, pp. 802–6

Cooper, James Fenimore, *The Oak Openings;, or, The Bee-Hunter*
(New York, 1848)

Cotton, William, *A Short and Simple Letter to Cottagers, from a Conservative
Bee-Keeper* (London, 1838)

Cotton, William, *My Bee Book* (London, 1842)

Crane, Eva, *A Book of Honey* (Oxford, 1980)

—, *Bees and Beekeeping: Science, Practice and World Resources*
(Oxford, 1990)

Day, Richard, *The Parliament of Bees* (London, 1697)

Ellison, Henry, *Stones from the Quarry* (London, 1875))

Evelyn, John, *Kalendarium Hortense; or, The Gardener's Almanac*
(London, 1664)

Frankum, Robert, *The Bee and the Wasp: A Fable* (London, 1832)

Frisch, Karl von, *The Dancing Bee: An Account of the Life and Senses
of the Honey Bee*, trans. Dora Lane (New York, 1955)

Gay, John, 'The Degenerate Bees', in *Fables* (London, 1795)

Gilbert, W. S., *Bab Ballads* (London, 1898)

Gilpin, George, *The Beehive of the Romish Church* (London, 1579)

Goodman, Godfrey, *The Fall of Man; or, The Corruption of Nature*
(London, 1616)

Grew, Nehemiah, *Musæum Regalis Societatis* (London, 1685)

Hall, Joseph, *Occasional Meditations* (London, 1630)

Hartog, Diana, *Polite to Bees: A Bestiary* (Toronto, 1992)

Hawkins, H., *Parthenia Sacra* (London, 1633)

Hayward, T. Curtis, *Bees of the Invisible: Creative Play and Divine Possession*
(London: The Guild of Pastoral Psychology, no. 206, n.d. [*c.* 1982])

Hesiod, *Works and Days* (Harmondsworth, 1985)

Hobbes, Thomas, *Leviathan* [1651] (Cambridge, 1991)

Hollander, John, ed., *American Poetry: The Nineteenth Cenutry*, 2 vols
(New York, 1993)

Hooke, Robert, *Micrographia* (London, 1665)

Isack , A. A., and H.-U. Reyer, 'Honeyguides and Honey Gatherers:
Interspecific Communication in a Symbiotic Relationship', *Science*, 243
(10 March 1989), pp. 1343–6

Jennings, Humphrey, *Pandæmonium* (London, 1985)

Jones, Gertrude, *Dictionary of Mythology, Folklore, and Symbols*, 3 vols
(New York, 1962)

Jonston, John, *An History of the Wonderful Things of Nature* (London, 1657)

Khalifman, I., *Bees* (Moscow, 1953)

Kidd, Sue Monk, *The Secret Life of Bees* (New York, 2002)

Kirk, Robert R., 'Bees', in *Poetry: Its Appreciation and Enjoyment*,
ed. Louis Untermeyer and Carter Davison (New York, 1934), p. 318

Klein, Richard, *Eat Fat* (London, 1997)

Lear, Edward, *A Book of Nonsense* (London, 1861)

Levett, John, *The Ordering of Bee; or, The True History of Managing
Them* (London, 1634)

Lévi-Strauss, Claude, *From Honey to Ashes: Introduction to a Science of
Mythology*, 2 vols, trans. John and Doreen Weightman (New York, 1973)
(originally published as *Mythologiques (Du Miel aux Cendres)*, 1966)

Lubbock, Sir John, *Ants, Bees, and Wasps* [1881] (London, 1915)

McClung, William A., *The Architecture of Paradise: Survivals of Eden
and Jerusalem* (Berkeley, CA, 1983)

McMahon, Thomas, *McKay's Bees* (London, 1979)

Maeterlinck, Maurice, *The Life of the Bee* [1901], trans. Alfred Sutro
(New York, 1924)

Mandelstam, Osip, *Selected Poems: A Necklace of Bees*, trans. Maria
Enzensberger (London, 1992)

—, *The Complete Poetry of Osip Emilevich Mandelstam*, trans. Burton Raffel
and Alla Burago (Albany, NY, 1973)

Marnix, Filips van, *De Roomsche Byen-korf* [1569], trans. John Still
(London, 1579)

Milne, A. A., *Winnie-the-Pooh* (London, 1926)

Mitterand, François, *The Wheat and the Chaff* (London, 1982)
(includes 'L'abeille et l'architecte')

Moffett, Thomas, *Insectorum sive minimorum animalium theatrum*,
in Edward Topsell, *The History of Fourfooted Beasts and Serpents . . .
whereunto is now added The Theater of Insects* (London, 1658)

Molan, Peter, 'The Anti-Bacterial Activity of Honey, Part I', *Bee World*, 73
(1992), pp. 5–28

Ovid, *Fasti*, trans. James Frazer (Cambridge, MA, 1931)

—, *Metamorphoses*, trans. Rolfe Humphries (Bloomington, IN, 1955)

Paley, Edward, 'Fable of the Bee-Hive', in *Reasons for Contentment
Addressed to the Labouring Part of the British Public* (London, 1831)

Pastan, Linda, 'The Death of the Bee', *Kenyon Review*, 20 (1998),
p. 73

Pausanias, *Description of Greece*, trans. W.H.S. Jones and H. A. Ormerod
(Cambridge, MA, 1965–6)

Pecke, Thomas, *Parnassi Puerperium* (London, 1659)

Pliny, *Historia Naturalis*, 10 vols, trans. H. Rackham (London and
Cambridge, MA, 1967)

Plot, Robert, *The Natural History of Oxfordshire* (London, 1677)

Purchas, Samuel, *A Treatise of Politicall Flying-Insects* (London, 1657)

Raleigh, Walter, *The History of the World* in *The Works of Sir Walter
Raleigh, Kt* (New York, 1829)

Ramirez, Juan Antonio, *The Beehive Metaphor: From Gaudí to Le Corbusier*
(London, 2000)

Ransome, Hilda M., *The Sacred Bee in Ancient Times and Folklore* [1937]
(Bridgwater, 1986)

Rolle, Richard, *The English Writings of Richard Rolle,* ed. Hope Emily Allen
    (Oxford, 1931)

Root, A. I., *The ABC and XYZ of Bee Culture* (Medina, OH, 1908)

Ruestow, Edward G., *The Microscope in the Dutch Republic: The Shaping
    of Discovery* (Cambridge, 1996)

Rusden, Moses, *A Further Discovery of Bees* (London, 1679)

Ruskin, John, *The Stones of Venice*, ed. J. G. Links (London, 1960)

Seneca, *De Clementia* in *Seneca's Morals Extracted in Three Books*,
    trans. Roger L'Estrange (London, 1679)

—, *Epistulae ad Lucilium,* 3 vols, trans. Richard M. Gummere
    (Cambridge, MA, 1917)

Steiner, Rudolf, *Bees,* trans. Thomas Brantz (Hudson, NY, 1998)

Sylvester, Joshua, trans., *The Divine Weeks and Works of Guillaume
    de Saluste du Bartas,* 2 vols, ed. Susan Snyder (Oxford, 1979)

Tacitus, *Annals*, trans. John Jackson (Cambridge, MA, 1970)

Tesauro, Emanuele, *Il Cannochiale Aristotelico* (Rome, 1664)

Thomas of Cantimpré, *Bonum Universale de Apibus* (*c.* 1259)

Tisdall, Caroline, *Joseph Beuys* (London, 1979)

Traynor, Joe, *Honey, the Gourmet Medicine* (Bakersfield, CA, 2002)

Tubach, Frederic, *Index Exemplorum: A Handbook of Medieval Religious
    Tales* (Helsinki, 1969)

Vanière, Jacques, *The Bees. A Poem*, trans. Arthur Murphy
    (London, 1799)

Varro, *Rerum Rusticarum*, trans. W. D. Hooper and H. B. Ash
    (Cambridge, MA, 1934)

Virgil, *Georgics*, trans. John Dryden (London, 1697)

Waterman, Charles E., *Apiatia: Little Essays on Honey-Makers*
    (Medina, OH, 1933)

Whitney, Geffrey, *A Choice of Emblems* (London, 1586)

Winston, Mark, *Killer Bees: The Africanized Honey Bee in the Americas*
    (Cambridge, MA, 1992).

Wither, George, *The Schollers Purgatory Discovered in the Stationers Common-wealth* (London, 1624)

Associations and Websites

ASSOCIATIONS

INTERNATIONAL BEE RESEARCH ASSOCIATION (IBRA)
www.ibra.org.uk

BRITISH BEEKEEPING ASSOCIATION (BBKA)
www.bbka.org.uk

AMERICAN BEEKEEPING FEDERATION (ABF)
www.abfnet.org

WEBSITES

NATIONAL HONEY BOARD (USA)
www.nhb.org

AMERICAN BEE JOURNAL
www.dadant.com

BEE CULTURE (MAGAZINE OF AMERICAN BEEKEEPING)
www.beeculture.com

BEEBASE (ANIMAL AND PLANT HEALTH AGENCY NATIONAL BEE UNIT)
www.nationalbeeunit.com

BUMBLEBEE CONSERVATION TRUST
www.bumblebeeconservation.org

LABORATORY OF APICULTURE AND SOCIAL INSECTS (LASI)
www.sussex.ac.uk/lasi

BEES-ONLINE
www.bees-online.com

www.beedata.com.

BEE FACTS
www.beehoo.com
Beekeeping directory

www.pollinator.org
Pollination homepage

www.ibiblio.org/bees/
Internet apiculture archive

www.jabootu.com
For bee movies

www.vegetus.org/honey/honey.htm
A vegan website opposed to beekeeping

Acknowledgements

Una apis nulla apis: this book is the work of many hands. It would not have been written without the encouragement and advice of Jonathan Burt, the *Animal* series editor. It is a pleasure also to thank Regina Davey and Lee Parsons, who introduced me to the delights of beekeeping, honey-extraction, and the quaffing of mead; Cecilia Royal for her exemplary research assistance; Michael Leaman, Harry Gilonis, Dave Hoek, Robert Williams and Vivian Constantinopoulos of Reaktion Books; and, for various witty contributions, jokes and criticisms, Bill Ashworth, Marion Berry, Tim Blanning, Anne Bradley, Susan Brigden, Eva Crane, Eberhard Duttra, Mark Godowski, Ulla Harmsen, Justine Hopkins, Dick Humphreys, Kevin Jackson, Kaptain Kidshow, Rebecca Kilner, Nick Laird, Kevin Loader, Herb Nadelhoffer, Barry Nisbet, Carole Parnaso, Angela Preston, Carol Preston, John Preston, Mark Preston, Michèle Royal, Elizabeth Shepherd-Barron, Nikolai Ssorin-Chaikov, John Strong, David Thompson, Bill Todd, Mary B. Wangerin, John Watts, Mary Lou Wehrli, and Clive Wilmer. The following libraries, museums, and organizations gave invaluable assistance: the Cambridge University Library, Bowdoin College Library, the British Library, the History of Advertising Trust Archive, the Bildarchiv Preussischer Kulturbesitz, Berlin, Staatliche Museen zu Berlin, the Musée des Beaux Arts, Dijon; as did the following individuals: Michael Cudlipp, Margaret Rose, and Sue Breakell (the History of Advertising Trust Archive), Richard Greene and Gunnar Madsen (The Bobs), Kim Flottum (*BeeCulture*), Anthony Rudolf (Menard Press), John Kinross (Bee Books New and Old), Ida Gnilšak (The Museum of Apiculture), Kate Kelly (Hasbro) and Bruce Bradley (Linda Hall Library).

Permission to reproduce texts and lyrics in whole or part are as follows: 'Take from my Palms', copyright © 2005 The Estate of Maria Enzenberger c/o Menard Press; 'Killer Bees' by The Bobs from *Songs for Tomorrow Morning*, Kaleidoscope Records, copyright © 1988 Richard Greene & Gunnar Madsen; Charles Waterman, *Apiatia: Little Essays on Honey-Makers*, copyright © A. I. Root Co., Publishers, Medina, Ohio; 'The Death of a Bee' from *Last Uncle* by Linda Pastan, copyright © 2002 by Linda Pastan, used by permission of W. W. Norton & Company, Inc.; 'Partake as doth the bee', 'The murmuring of bees has ceased' and 'I taste a liquor never brewed' reprinted by permission of the publishers and the Trustees of Amherst College from *The Poems of Emily Dickinson*, Thomas H. Johnson, ed., Cambridge, Mass.: The Belknap Press of Harvard University Press, copyright © 1951, 1955, 1979, 1983 by the President and Fellows of Harvard College.

Photo Acknowledgements

The author and publishers wish to express their thanks to the following sources of illustrative material and/or permission to reproduce it:

Photos by the author: pp. 52, 64, 110 (left), 113 (top), 126, 175; photos courtesy of the estate of Michael Ayrton: p. 107; photos by permission of Bee Books New and Old, Little Dewchurch, Herefordshire HR2 6PP: pp. 10, 11, 30 (left), 34, 36, 66; photo courtesy of Boosey & Hawkes Music Publishers Ltd: p. 116; British Library, London: p. 47 (BL MS Add 15950, f. 142; photo, British Library Reproductions); British Museum, London (photo by permission of the British Museum, London): p. 122 (top); photos by permission of the Syndics of Cambridge University Library: pp. 9, 22, 24, 25, 28, 37, 38, 39, 42 (top left), 43, 44, 49, 56, 57, 56, 58 (top), 61, 71, 73, 88, 89, 90, 110 (right), 112, 117, 130, 131, 139, 140, 141; photos courtesy of Eva Crane: pp. 29 (middle, right), 84 (top); photo courtesy of *Dialogue: A Journal of Mormon Thought*: p. 129; photo courtesy of Eberhard Düttra: p. 14 (top left); reproduced courtesy of the artist (Ian Hamilton Finlay): p. 78; photo by permission of the History of Advertising Trust: p. 92; Kunsthistoriches Museum, Vienna (photo by permission of the Kunsthistoriches Museum, Vienna): p. 72; photos Library of Congress, Washington, DC: p. 42 top right (Prints and Photographs Division, photograph from the records of the National Child Labor Committee, LC-DIG-NCLC-00316, photo Lewis Wickes Hine), 59 (Prints and Photographs Division, Gottscho-Schleisner Collection, LC-G613-72127), 60 (Prints and Photographs Division, Theatrical Poster Collection, var 0907), 146 (Prints and Photographs Division, British Cartoon Collection,

LC-USZ62-132979), 155 (Prints and Photographs Division, Farm Security Administration – Office of War Information Photograph Collection, LC-USF34-014113-D), 158 (Prints and Photographs Division, Farm Security Administration – Office of War Information Photograph Collection, LC-USW33-024218-C, photo National Council of American-Soviet Friendship, New York); photos by permission of the Linda Hall Library of Science, Engineering & Technology, Kansas City, MO: pp. 96, 122 (foot), 123; Musée des Beaux-Arts, Dijon (photo François Jay/© Musée des Beaux-Arts, Dijon): p. 90; photo by permission of the Museum of Apiculture, Radovljica, Slovenia: p. 84 (foot); National Gallery, London (photo by permission of the National Gallery, London): p. 70; photo courtesy of the National Honey Board www.honey.com]: p. 137; photos Rex Features: pp. 6 (Rex Features/Organic Picture Library, 366312A), 100 (Rex Features/RESO, 424222a), 104 (Rex Features/Chris Martin Bahr, 346821A), 113 foot (Rex Features/Harry Goodwin, 325969M), 152 (Rex Features/Ville Myllynen (462108E), 174 (Rex Features/ Greg Williams, 259319a); photos Roger-Viollet, courtesy of Rex Features: pp. 33 (10225-4/RV-115331H), 76 (top) (Collection Roger-Viollet, 2016-15/RV-925011); Romper Room © 2005 Hasbro, used with permission: p. 142; photo courtesy of A. I. Root Publishers: p. 29; photos by kind permission of Prof. Mandyam V. Srinivasan: p. 21; photo by permission of the Staatliche Museen, Berlin: p. 149; reproduced from the original held by the Department of Special Collections of the University Libraries of Notre Dame, Notre Dame, Indiana (photo by permission of Notre Dame University): p. 74.

Index

Page numbers in *italics* indicate illustrations